The

Country Cooking
Book

The
Beatrix Potter™
Country Cooking
Book

Sara Paston-Williams

Photography by Ian O'Leary

CLAREMONT/WARNE

(Beatrix Potter's Country Cooking Book)

CLAREMONT BOOKS
in association with Frederick Warne

Published by the Penguin Group
27 Wright's Lane, London W8 5TZ, England
Penguin Books USA Inc., 375 Hudson Street, New York, New York 10014, USA
Penguin Books Australia Ltd, Ringwood, Victoria, Australia
Penguin Books Canada Ltd, 10 Alcorn Avenue, Toronto, Ontario, Canada M4V 3B2
Penguin Books (NZ) Ltd, 182-190 Wairau Road, Auckland 10, New Zealand
Penguin Books Ltd, Registered Offices: Harmondsworth, Middlesex, England

Claremont Books, an imprint of the Godfrey Cave Group, 42 Bloomsbury Street, London WC1B 3QJ

First published 1991 as *Beatrix Potter's Country Cooking* by Frederick Warne
This edition first published 1995
1 3 5 7 9 10 8 6 4 2

ISBN 1 85471 6182

Design by Ronnie Wilkinson
Colour origination by Anglia Graphics Ltd, Bedford
Printed and bound in Great Britain by
BPC Hazell Books Ltd
A member of
The British Printing Company Ltd

*A*CKNOWLEDGEMENTS

The author and publishers would like to express thanks to the following:

For assistance with research and recipes
Mollie Green, Anvil Cottage, Near Sawrey; Harry and Kate Fellows, Ashdown Smokers, near Waberthwaite; Jean Butterworth; Lynn Hadley, Cedar Manor Hotel, Windermere; Tom and Janie Smith and Joan Griffiths of Gwaenynog and Denbigh Farmhouse Ices; Gillian Fletcher, High Green Gate, Near Sawrey, and Michael Fletcher; Nigel Woodhouse and staff, Hawkshead Trout Farm, Esthwaite; John and Margaret Williams, Lakefield Hotel, Sawrey; Neville Talbot and staff, Lakeside Hotel, Newby Bridge; Richard and Eleanor Quinlan, The Mill, Mungrisdale; Francis Coulson, Brian Sack and staff, Sharrow Bay Hotel, Ullswater; Stewart and Janice Greaves, Sheila's Cottage, Ambleside; Willow Taylor; Philip Broadley, family and staff, Tower Bank Arms, Near Sawrey; Janet and Michael Greenwood, Tullythwaite House, Underbarrow; Peter and Sue Dixon, White Moss House Hotel, Rydal Water; Richard Woodall, Waberthwaite

For permission to reproduce original Beatrix Potter illustrations and historic photographs
Trustees of the Linder Collection, Book Trust; National Art Library, Victoria and Albert Museum; Pierpont Morgan Library, New York; Frederick Warne Archive; private collectors

For contributing to the production of this book
Ricky Turner and Judy Bugg, home economists; Marian Price, stylist; Ian Garlick and Melissa Favot, for photographic assistance; Jennie Walters and Roni Durie for editorial assistance

Contents

$\mathscr{I}$NTRODUCTION

Beatrix Potter was born in 1866 in London, although she was to write seventy-five years later, 'Our descent – our interests and our joy was in the north country.' Her parents were well-to-do and middle-class. Like so many children in a wealthy Victorian household, she led a rather lonely life, confined to the nursery for most of the day. However, there were outings to look forward to, especially visits to her grandmother's house, Camfield Place in Hertfordshire, which delighted the young Beatrix. It was here she first tasted farm produce – fresh milk, new-laid eggs and home-made bread – which she was to enjoy all her life.

Beatrix and her younger brother Bertram were also frequently taken on holidays. The Potter family spent at least three months of every year in Scotland or, later, the English Lake District. Here the children discovered the simple delights of country living and the beauty of the wild life about them. Animals became Beatrix's constant companions and she started to draw and paint them in meticulous detail.

Above: From The Tale of Peter Rabbit

Below: Beatrix, her brother Bertram and her mother picnicking on Ifracombe beach during their West Country holiday in April 1883. Her father Rupert, a keen amateur photographer, was behind the camera

Above: Salmon-fishing was a favourite pastime in Scotland where the Potters and their guests spent many summers. This photograph, taken after a fishing trip, shows Mr and Mrs Potter, Lady Millais and young Beatrix with the successful catch.

During the Potters' first visit to the Lake District, while they were staying at Wray Castle on the shore of Windermere, Beatrix met Canon Hardwicke Rawnsley, who at the time was crusading for the formation of a National Trust to buy and preserve places of natural beauty and historic interest. His chief concern was the threat to the Lake District from developers of railways, factories and housing estates, and he had a considerable effect on the sixteen-year-old Beatrix. Later, she was to continue his work on her own behalf by buying farm land and cottages in the wild and beautiful landscape she had chosen as her home, with the aim of preserving them for ever.

It was also from Canon Rawnsley, a published author of poems and sonnets himself, that she received the encouragement in 1901 to risk a modest venture in privately publishing her first 'little book' for children. *The Tale of Peter Rabbit* was the first and

is still the most popular in the series of illustrated tales known and loved by millions of children – and adults – all over the world. It was these books, published by Frederick Warne, that provided Beatrix with the money to buy farms and land in the Lake District, while she continued to write and paint and commute from her parents' home in London.

After the death in 1905 of Beatrix's fiancé, Norman Warne, she became more determined to get away altogether from London and she spent as much time as she could at her farm, Hill Top, in the village of Near Sawrey. Eight years later, she married her solicitor from nearby Hawkshead, a kindly, 'real north-country man', and she became Mrs William Heelis. She moved permanently to the Lake District and at the age of forty-seven she acquired her own kitchen at Castle Cottage. 'Nothing smart, just bare flags, a scrubbed table and ordinary ladder-backed chairs,' recalls a villager. Beatrix had never cooked for herself and had no experience in the kitchen, but she and Willie took a keen interest in food. 'There are probably more disputes over bacon and plain pota-toes than any other eatable,' Beatrix observed in the

Above: The view from the roof of Hill Top illustrated in The Tale of Samuel Whiskers

Above: A village kitchen in The Tale of The Pie and The Patty-Pan
Left: Beatrix Potter outside Hill Top in 1913

early months of their marriage. 'I can do both – and very little else!' Together, they embarked on what she described in a letter as 'a large and arduous campaign of cookery'. By the first Christmas after her marriage, Mrs Heelis had made progress. 'The messes – mingled with really elegant suppers – which William and I cooked . . . are most remarkable. William took a turn at pastry *à la* Mrs Beeton, but I am of the opinion she recommends the use – or misuse – of more butter than is justified by results. What we do really well are roasts and vegetables. We cooked and ate a turkey and several other birds.'

The Heelises enjoyed simple traditional country dishes using fresh produce. The farm, 'old-fashioned farm garden' and orchard provided nearly all they needed – sheep, cattle, pigs, hutch rabbits, ducks, turkeys, chickens, eggs, dairy produce, vegetables, herbs and fruit, whilst Willie was keen on shooting and fishing and Beatrix loved collecting wild plants, fruits and nuts from the surrounding countryside.

However, they were both very busy people. Beatrix became a fully-fledged farmer – the biggest sheep farmer in the Lake District – as well as a writer and painter, and so they normally had help in the kitchen and the garden. Their marriage was most successful and they continued to lead very full and happy lives.

After her death in 1943, Beatrix Potter's 'dear farms and sheep', fourteen in number, as well as many smaller cottages, passed into the hands of the National Trust, who continue her work of preserving the beauty and traditions of Lakeland. After spending so much time there doing the research for this book, I can understand Beatrix Potter's passion for the place that made her 'feel so very well' and gave her 'a school-boy's appetite' she was 'almost ashamed of'. It had the same effect on me, and that's *my* excuse for devouring so many traditional Lakeland breakfasts!

Above: From The Tale of Mrs. Tittlemouse

Below: Beatrix Potter at a country show in the 1930s, with prize-winning sheep

10

Above: Anna Maria runs past the Hill Top dresser in The Tale of Samuel Whiskers

Below: From The Tale of Johnny Town-Mouse

I found the Lakelanders extremely kind and welcoming and very willing to share their favourite recipes with me, whether they were running a tiny guest-house or a very smart hotel. The local produce is certainly of an excellent standard and the food quite delicious, and so I hope you enjoy this collection of recipes.

Beatrix Potter's first home is open to the public during the summer months and visitors to Hill Top will feel the presence of Beatrix Potter and 'friends' everywhere. Her clogs made by Charlie Brown of Hawkshead are waiting by the fire for her to come striding in wearing the familiar old herringbone costume of Herdwick wool and floppy trilby-style hat. Perhaps she is still walking on the fells above Troutbeck Farm with 'the company of gentle sheep and wild flowers and singing water'? I like to think so.

SARA PASTON-WILLIAMS

MEASUREMENTS AND GLOSSARY

Throughout this book the ingredients for each receipe are given in metric, imperial and American measures.
e.g. 50 g (2 oz/¼ cup) butter

Note that the British standard tablespoon, the British standard pint and the British fluid ounce are all larger than their American equivalents. References to tablespoons, pints and fl oz indicate the British measures unless specifically stated. e.g. 2 (3 US) tablespoons olive oil

GLOSSARY OF BRITISH AND AMERICAN TERMS

with suggested substitutes for American readers

back bacon	Canadian bacon
bacon rashers	bacon slices
beetroot	beet
bicarbonate of soda	baking soda
black pudding	blood sausage
caster sugar	granulated sugar
celeriac	celery root
chemist shop	drugstore
chicory	Belgian endive
cling film	plastic wrap
clotted cream	thick, rich cream
cooking apples	tart apples e.g. Granny Smith
cucumber	Note that British cucumbers are generally about twice as big as the American vegetables of the same name

damsons	Substitute small purple plums (will not be as tart)
dark treacle	molasses
Demerara sugar	light brown sugar
double cream	whipping cream
draining spoon	slotted spoon
fluted flan ring	fluted tart pan
glacé cherries	candied cherries
glucose	dextrose, corn sugar, grape sugar
golden syrup	Can be found in some specialty food stores, or substitute corn syrup
granary flour	a type of wholemeal flour
grater	shredder
greaseproof paper	parchment paper
Greek-style yoghurt	rich, creamy yogurt

green bacon........................unsmoked bacon
Guinness............................Can be found in some specialty liquor stores, or substitute dark beer

hard-boiled eggs.................hard-cooked eggs

icing sugar.........................powdered sugar

Jerusalem artichoke.............sunchoke

marrow..............................vegetable marrow, marrow squash. Substitute 4–6 large zucchini for 1 medium marrow
mince................................grind
minced meat.......................ground meat
mixed spice........................pumpkin pie or apple pie spice
muslin...............................cheesecloth

natural yoghurt..................plain yogurt

oatcakes............................Can be found at some specialty food stores

palette knife......................metal spatula
peppermint essence............peppermint extract
petit pois...........................tiny peas
pie plate............................shallow pie pan or ovenproof glass plate
pie veal.............................veal stewmeat
plain chocolate...................semisweet chocolate

plain flour..........................all-purpose flour
polythene bag.....................plastic bag
prawns..............................tiny shrimp

red pepper..........................red bell pepper

salad rocket........................arugula
sandwich tin.......................layer cake pan
scone topping......................biscuit topping or crust
self-raising flour.................If unavailable, substitute 1½ teaspoons baking powder and ⅛ teaspoon salt to every 1 cup all-purpose flour
Seville oranges...................bitter oranges
soured cream......................sour cream
spring onions.....................green onions
standard eggs.....................medium eggs
stem ginger........................preserved ginger
stone.................................fruit pit or seed
sultanas.............................golden raisins
swedes..............................rutabagas
Swiss roll...........................jelly roll

tomato purée......................tomato paste
top and tail........................trim

vanilla essence...................vanilla extract. Note that vanilla extract is not as concentrated as British vanilla essence and so a larger quantity has to be used to achieve an equivalent flavour

13

Starters

Spring Soup 16

Rich Game Soup with Elderberry Wine 16

Creamy Turnip and Sage Soup 17

Chilled Pea and Peppermint Soup 18

Wild Mushroom, Marjoram and Madeira Soup 18

Solway Potted Shrimps 19

Smoked Sea Trout Pâté 20

Scottish Smoked Salmon and Crab Parcels 21

Morecambe Shrimp Tarts 22

Daisy Pineapple with Garlic Cheese 24

Creamy Spinach Pâté 24

Potted Venison 25

Smoked Herdwick Macon with Rhubarb
and Angelica Mousse 25

SPRING SOUP

---

*Helen Beatrix Potter was born in 1866 in a
tall, four-storeyed house in Kensington, London:
Number 2, Bolton Gardens. She spent much of her
childhood in the nursery on the top floor, in the care of a
nurse and later, a governess. There were at least five
servants employed at Bolton Gardens. The dinner parties
were certainly elaborate; on 7 May, 1875, for instance, the
menu was 'Spring Soup, Salmon, Sweetbreads, Lobster
Cutlets, Spring Chickens, Ham, Roast Lamb, Ducklings
and Peas, Mousseline Pudding, Jelly, Cherry Ice and Brown
Bread Ice'. Beatrix detested these stultifying dinners and
yearned for plain simple fare.*
*Spring Soup à la Mrs. Beeton, and probably
2 Bolton Gardens, was made with green peas, lettuce,
onions, 'a very small bunch of parsley and a little chervil'
and thickened with numerous egg yolks.*
*This is a much simpler country recipe in which
any combination of green spring vegetables and plants may
be used, including very young nettles.*

50 g (2 oz/¼ cup) butter
250 g (8 oz) leeks, thinly sliced
250 g (8 oz) potatoes, finely chopped
1 litre (2 pints/5 cups) chicken stock
250 g (8 oz) Swiss chard leaves or spinach
125 g (4 oz) wild or garden sorrel
50 g (2 oz) watercress
Salt and freshly milled black pepper
150 ml (¼ pint/⅔ cup) cream, yoghurt or buttermilk
Chopped watercress, to garnish

Melt the butter in a large saucepan and stir in the
leeks and potatoes. Cover with a lid and cook gently
for about 10 minutes. Add the stock, bring to the boil
and then reduce the heat, cover and simmer for about
20 minutes, or until the potatoes are soft.

While the soup is cooking, wash the Swiss chard or
spinach, sorrel and watercress, discarding any tough
stalks. Shake dry, then chop finely.

Add the chopped green vegetables to the cooked
soup and simmer for just a few minutes more to heat
through, then purée in a blender or food processor.
Return to a clean pan and season to taste. Add the
cream, yoghurt or buttermilk and reheat very gently,
without boiling.

Serve hot or cold, garnished with a little chopped
watercress. (Serves 6)

RICH GAME SOUP WITH ELDERBERRY WINE

---

*Although Beatrix Potter's childhood was mainly spent in
London, she did have some taste of country life. The whole
family, plus servants, would decamp to the countryside for
a three-month holiday every summer. Beatrix's father,
Rupert, would rent a large house and estate, usually in
Scotland, and spend time with his guests hunting, shooting
and fishing. The Potter family would frequently have
enjoyed game soup made from the older game birds and
tougher parts of venison.*

450 g (1 lb) neck of venison
or a 900 g (2 lb) grouse or pheasant
125 g (4 oz/½ cup) butter
1 large onion, chopped
1 medium leek, chopped
2 sticks of celery, chopped
1 large carrot, chopped
1 medium parsnip, chopped
2 bay leaves
1 ½ teaspoons chopped fresh thyme
or ½ teaspoon dried
2 cloves of garlic, crushed
1.8 litres (3 pints/7½ cups) cold water
1½ (2 US) tablespoons tomato purée
250 g (8 oz/2¾ cups) sliced field mushrooms
4 whole cloves
Salt and freshly milled black pepper
50 g (2 oz/⅓ cup) plain flour
150 ml (¼ pint/⅔ cup) elderberry wine,
red wine or port
Croutons of fried brown bread, to garnish
Chopped fresh chervil or parsley, to garnish

Cut the venison into 5 cm (2 in) cubes, discarding the gristle. If using grouse or pheasant, cut the bird into small portions, including all the bone.

Melt half the butter in a large pan and fry the meat until brown all over. Remove with a slotted spoon and put to one side. Gradually add the onion, leek, celery, carrot and parsnip to the pan and fry them over a good heat, taking care to brown them without burning and stirring all the time. Put the meat back into the pan and add the bay leaves, thyme and garlic. Pour in the water and bring quickly to the boil. Remove any scum which rises on the surface, then stir in the tomato purée, mushrooms and cloves. Season well, then cover with a lid and simmer over a very low heat for about 2 hours, or until the meat is very tender.

Drain off the stock and strain it through a fine sieve. Leave to cool a little. Remove and discard the bay leaves, cloves and all the bones from the remaining meat and vegetables, then put this mixture in a blender or food processor to make a thick purée.

Melt the remaining butter in a large clean pan and stir in the flour. Cook for a few minutes until golden brown, then gradually stir in the elderberry wine, red wine or port and about 300 ml (½ pint/1¼ cups) of reserved stock. Bring to simmering point, stirring all the time, then blend in the meat and vegetable purée and enough stock to make a thickish soup. Taste and adjust seasoning if necessary, then cook for about 15 minutes over a low heat until ready to serve.

Serve in warm bowls, garnished with small croutons of fried brown bread and a little chopped fresh chervil or parsley. (Serves 6)

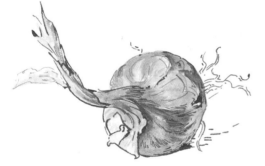

CREAMY TURNIP AND SAGE SOUP

From the mid 1880s onwards the Potter family began from time to time to spend their long summer holiday in the English Lake District rather than Scotland. From her earliest visits to the Lake District, Beatrix Potter loved the local agricultural shows. In 1896 she wrote in her journal: 'The only prize we took was for common turnips.' Much later, when Beatrix was married and living in the Lake District, she was to grow 'common turnips' herself. Small white turnips may be used to make this soup, based on a recipe given to me by Jean Butterworth of Easedale, Grasmere.

50 g (2 oz/¼ cup) duck fat or butter
1 medium onion, chopped
450 g (1 lb) turnips, chopped
1 large potato, chopped
1 litre (2 pints/5 cups) duck or chicken stock
Salt and freshly milled black pepper
6 fresh sage leaves
6 tablespoons (½ cup) cream, natural yoghurt
or buttermilk
6 purple sage leaves, to garnish

Melt the fat in a large saucepan and add the onion. Cover with a lid and cook gently until the onion is soft, but not coloured. Add the turnips and potato and stir well into the buttery juices. Continue to cook gently for a further 10 minutes, then pour in the stock. Bring to the boil, then cover and simmer very gently for about 20 minutes, or until the vegetables are soft. Season with salt and pepper, then liquidise with the fresh sage leaves. Taste and add more seasoning if necessary. Return to a clean pan and reheat gently.

Serve with swirls of cream, yoghurt or buttermilk and garnished with sage leaves. Accompany with crusty homemade bread (see page 125) or savoury cheese or herb scones (see page 131). Serve for lunch with thick slices of fresh crusty bread, generously buttered and piled high with peppery watercress. (Serves 6)

CHILLED PEA AND PEPPERMINT SOUP

*One of the books that Beatrix Potter wrote
and illustrated in the Lake District is* The Tale
of Johnny Town-Mouse. *In the story it is a surfeit
of fresh garden peas that leads to poor Timmy Willie going
to town by mistake in a hamper. Timmy Willie's garden
was in Near Sawrey, where Beatrix had her home, and the
town mice lived in Hawkshead in the home of a
Mrs Bolton, who received vegetables from the village of
Sawrey each week and sent back laundry. The cook in
the story was based on a Mrs Rogerson, who cooked for
Beatrix and her husband Willie Heelis at Castle Cottage,
their Lake District home.*

450 g (1 lb) frozen petit pois
2 level teaspoons sugar
1 clove of garlic, crushed
10 small sprigs of fresh peppermint or spearmint
Juice of 1 lemon
300 ml (½ pint/1¼ cups) single cream
600 ml (1 pint/2½ cups) cold chicken stock
150 ml (¼ pint/⅔ cup) soured cream or
natural yoghurt
Chopped fresh chives, to garnish

Put the peas in a saucepan with the sugar, crushed
garlic and peppermint. Toss over a low heat without
adding any water until the peas are tender. Leave to
cool, then add the lemon juice. Liquidise the soup in
a blender or food processor until smooth.

Stir in the single cream, then add enough stock to
make the soup the consistency of single cream. Chill
well in the fridge, preferably overnight.

Serve in individual chilled bowls or glasses, decorated with a swirl of soured cream and a sprinkling
of chopped chives, or serve hot with crusty bread.
(Serves 6)

WILD MUSHROOM, MARJORAM AND MADEIRA SOUP

*Beatrix Potter's great interest in fungi and
lichen began in her childhood, when the family
stayed at Dalguise House in Perthshire, Scotland, for their
three-month summer holiday. It was here
that she met Charlie McIntosh, the 'Perthshire
Naturalist', whose work can still be seen at the Perth
Museum. Much later, Beatrix met up again with Charlie,
and his quiet approval of her studies encouraged her
enormously. She became extremely knowledgeable and
produced over 300 drawings of which any mycologist
would be proud today. Beatrix also enjoyed collecting
edible fungi, for another purpose!
Many varieties of wild mushrooms (such as field, horse,
parasols, chanterelles, puff-balls) are now sold
commercially in season. If you are collecting mushrooms
in the wild, take care to pick only those you can
positively identify.*

125 g (4 oz/½ cup) butter
1 medium onion, chopped
1 clove of garlic, crushed
350 g (12 oz) wild mushrooms
1½ (2 US) tablespoons chopped fresh marjoram
or 1½ teaspoons (1 US tablespoon) dried
900 ml (1½ pints/3¾ cups) chicken stock
50 g (2 oz/¼ cup) plain flour
300 ml (½ pint/1¼ cups) milk or single cream
6 tablespoons (½ cup) Madeira or sherry
Salt and freshly milled black pepper
Freshly grated nutmeg
150 ml (¼ pint/⅔ cup) soured cream
or natural yoghurt
Sprigs of fresh marjoram, to garnish

Melt half the butter in a large pan and add the onion
and garlic. Cook gently until soft.

Meanwhile, wipe the mushrooms with a damp
cloth (do not wash them) and slice roughly. Stir into
the onion mixture and fry at a higher temperature for
1 minute. Reduce the heat again, add the marjoram

Solway potted shrimps and smoked sea trout pâté at Sheila's Kitchen, Ambleside

and pour in the stock. Cover the pan and simmer for 10–15 minutes. Purée this mushroom mixture in a blender or food processor. If possible, transfer the purée into a covered container and leave in the fridge for a couple of days, for the flavours to mellow.

Melt the remaining butter in a pan and stir in the flour. Cook for a few minutes over a gentle heat, then gradually stir in the milk or cream. Cook gently until thick and smooth. Heat the mushroom mixture in a large pan, then gradually stir in the white sauce and the Madeira or sherry. Season to taste with salt, pepper and nutmeg. Serve hot with swirls of soured cream or yoghurt and garnished with fresh marjoram.

Accompany with thick slices of crusty wholemeal bread or rolls. (Serves 6)

*S*OLWAY POTTED SHRIMPS

The tiny shrimps from Morecambe Bay and the Solway are exported all over the world. Shelling is still done by hand, as it was in Beatrix Potter's day, and the only change to the shrimp industry since then is that the nets are pulled through the shallow water by tractors instead of horses. The shrimps have been potted in tiny factories along this coast in the same way for years and the Potters must have tasted them many times during their summer holidays in the Lake District.

This Cumbrian delicacy is made daily in the kitchen at Sheila's Cottage in Ambleside, and their recipe is given overleaf.

125 g (4 oz/½ cup) butter
575 g (1¼ lb) shrimps, shelled
½ teaspoon sea salt
Large pinch of freshly grated nutmeg
Large pinch of ground mace
Freshly milled black pepper
50 g (2 oz/¼ cup) clarified butter
Watercress, to garnish

Heat the butter in a pan until it just melts. Add the shrimps and sauté in the butter for a few minutes until they are coated, taking care not to break them up. Season with salt, nutmeg, mace and black pepper to taste and mix well. Pack into small pots and leave to set.

Heat up the clarified butter and pour over the top of each dish to seal the contents. (This way they will keep in a cold place for several days.)

Garnish with watercress and serve as a starter with hot toasted wholemeal bread, using the clarified shrimp butter to spread on the toast, or with brown bread and butter, or with oatcakes. Alternatively, serve for lunch *à la* Sheila's Cottage with lemon mayonnaise, fresh granary bread and a crisp seasonal salad. (Serves 6–8)

SMOKED SEA TROUT PÂTÉ

This super pâté is regularly on the menu at Sheila's Cottage in the Lake District town of Ambleside. Serve as a starter or for a light lunch.

450 g (1 lb) smoked sea trout or smoked trout, skinned and boned
50 g (2 oz/¼ cup) butter
125 g (4 oz) cream cheese
2 (3 US) tablespoons soured cream or natural yoghurt
Juice of ½ a lemon
½ teaspoon ground mace
Sea salt and freshly milled black pepper
1 tablespoon horseradish cream
75 g (3 oz/⅓ cup) clarified butter (optional)
Sprigs of fresh dill or fennel, to garnish

Purée the trout in a blender or food processor, then gradually add the remaining ingredients, except the clarified butter, and purée to a smooth paste. Taste and adjust seasoning as necessary, then spoon into a pretty pot or dish. Pour over a film of clarified butter if you wish and leave to set.

Take out of the fridge at least 1 hour before needed. Garnish with sprigs of fresh dill or fennel and serve with freshly toasted wholemeal bread. (Serves 6–8)

*S*COTTISH SMOKED SALMON AND CRAB PARCELS

*In addition to their three-month summer
holiday spent in Scotland or the Lake District,
the Potter family used to leave London for two or three
weeks each April, while the spring cleaning was in hand, to
stay in seaside hotels in the West Country.
Here, a speciality from Scotland is combined with
one from the West Country to make a very simple,
yet glamorous, starter.*

Sunflower or safflower oil
6 sprigs of fresh dill or chervil
About 250 g (8 oz) smoked salmon, very thinly sliced
175–250 g (6–8 oz) crab meat, mixed white and brown
Salt and freshly milled black pepper
150 ml (¼ pint/⅔ cup) soured cream
or natural yoghurt
A little of the white part of a leek, finely chopped
A few salad leaves, to garnish (optional)

Lightly oil 6 small ramekin dishes and place a sprig of fresh dill or chervil at the bottom of each, then line the dishes with the smoked salmon, letting a little surplus hang over the rims.

Season the crab meat to taste and mix well. Divide it between the dishes and fold the ends of the smoked salmon over to encase it completely. Cover with cling film and refrigerate for at least 4 hours to allow the flavours to blend.

Meanwhile, pour the soured cream or yoghurt into a small basin and add a little chopped leek. Cover and leave in the fridge for the flavours to infuse.

Just before serving, remove the ramekins from the fridge and bring them to room temperature. Run a palette knife around the edge of each dish and unmould the smoked salmon and crab parcels on to individual plates. Spoon a little of the leek sauce on to each plate and decorate with a few salad leaves if you wish.

Eat with thin, buttered brown bread or warmed oatcakes if you are serving as a starter, or with chunks of wholemeal bread for lunch. (Serves 6)

Lyme Regis, sketched by Beatrix Potter in about 1904, during one of her West Country seaside holidays

MORECAMBE SHRIMP TARTS

Beatrix Potter often took her favourite animals away with her when she travelled. In a letter to her publisher, Norman Warne, from her uncle's house in Wales, she confided, 'I am also accompanied by Mrs Tiggy [her hedgehog] carefully concealed – my aunt cannot endure animals!'
In one of her special picture letters from Wales to Norman's young niece, Winifred Warne (dated 6 September, 1905), she wrote: 'I think I am going to the sea-side on Saturday. I wonder if I shall find any crabs and shells and shrimps. Mrs Tiggy-winkle won't eat shrimps; I think it is very silly of her, she will eat worms and beetles, and I am sure that shrimps would be much nicer.'
These delicious shrimp tartlets are regularly on the menu at the Sharrow Bay Hotel on Ullswater, using potted shrimps from Morecambe Bay. One of the rooms at this famous hotel, run by Francis Coulson and Brian Sack, has been named after Beatrix Potter.

For the pastry

225 g (8 oz/1½ cups) plain flour
1 dessertspoon icing sugar
Pinch of salt
150 g (5 oz/¾ cup) butter
1 egg, beaten
A little cold water

For the filling

4 cartons potted shrimps
1 small onion, very finely chopped
2 (3 US) tablespoons plain flour
300 ml (½ pint/1¼ cups) single cream
¼ cucumber (½ American cucumber), finely chopped, drained
Salt and freshly milled black pepper
Freshly grated nutmeg
Grated rind and juice of 1 lemon
A few salad leaves, lemon and cucumber slices and sprigs of fresh fennel or dill, to garnish

Instead of buying potted shrimps, you can, if you wish, make this recipe using half the quantity of the Solway potted shrimps described on pages 19–20.

To make the pastry, sieve the flour, icing sugar and salt into a bowl. Lightly rub the butter into the flour until the mixture acquires a sand-like texture. Gradually add the beaten egg and a little water to make a pliable dough and knead very lightly. Leave to rest in the fridge for about 30 minutes before using.

Pre-heat the oven to 200°C (400°F, gas mark 6) including a baking sheet.

Roll out the prepared pastry and use to line six 11-cm (4-in) individual fluted tart tins with removable bases. Line with greaseproof paper or foil and weigh down with baking beans. Place on the pre-heated baking sheet and bake blind for 15 minutes, then remove the lining paper and beans and bake the pastry for a further 10–15 minutes until pale golden and crisp.

While the pastry cases are cooking, prepare the filling. Warm the potted shrimps in a pan until the butter falls from them, then remove the shrimps with a slotted spoon and reserve on one side.

Cook the onion in the shrimp butter until soft and transparent. Stir in the flour and cook for a few minutes, then add the cream. Stir over a low heat until the sauce is smooth and thick, then add the reserved shrimps and cucumber. Heat through gently and season to taste with salt, pepper, nutmeg, lemon rind and lemon juice.

Just before serving, place a warm pastry case on each of 6 small plates and fill with the shrimp mixture. Garnish with a few salad leaves, twists of lemon and cucumber and sprigs of fresh herbs.

The pastry cases may be cooked and cooled completely before wrapping and storing in an airtight tin until needed. (Serves 6)

Morecambe shrimp tart, served in the dining-room at the Sharrow Bay Hotel, Ullswater

DAISY PINEAPPLE WITH GARLIC CHEESE

On Thursday, 21 June, 1883, when Beatrix
Potter was seventeen, she painted the pineapple
bought for that evening's dinner party: 'Small dinner,
am painting the pineapple, etc. Mr Halliday was cutting it
up on a plate behind me. I felt fit to kick
under my chair. I thought there would be none left.'
Typically, the 'etc.' included her pet lizard, Judy, brought
back from a holiday in Ilfracombe.

1 large ripe pineapple
1 clove of garlic, crushed with a little sea salt
175 g (6 oz) low-fat soft curd or cream cheese
or fromage frais
1 scant tablespoon chopped fresh parsley
1 scant tablespoon chopped fresh chervil
Daisy flowers and leaves, to garnish

Cut off the leafy crown of the pineapple and cut the
fruit into 6 slices. Remove the skin of the pineapple
and snip out the brown 'pines' and the central cores.
Cut each slice in half, then arrange 2 halves in an
overlapping line on 6 small plates, pouring over any
excess juice. Beat the crushed garlic into the cheese
with the parsley and chervil. Divide the cheese
between the 6 plates, arranging a portion down the
centre of the pineapple slices. Separate the daisy
flowers from their stalks and make sure they are
insect-free, then arrange them around the cheese,
with a few small leaves.
  Serve slightly chilled. (Serves 6)

CREAMY SPINACH PÂTÉ

Spinach beet, or perpetual spinach, seakale
beet and Swiss chard are coarser in texture than
true spinach, but they grow well in the north of Britain.
The stems of Swiss chard are firmer than those of spinach
and spinach beet, but it is a lovely vegetable.
The leaves can be cooked in the same way as spinach,
while the rather sweet stems should be cooked separately
and served with butter or a white sauce.
This pâté is popular even with those who insist
they don't like spinach!

450 g (1 lb) spinach, spinach beet
or Swiss chard leaves
1 small onion, finely chopped
1 heaped tablespoon finely chopped fresh parsley
1½ teaspoons chopped fresh tarragon
or ½ teaspoon dried
2 hard-boiled eggs
4 sardines or 1 tin anchovies
2 (3 US) tablespoons double cream, Greek-style
yoghurt or mayonnaise
Salt and freshly milled black pepper
Slices of hard-boiled egg and rolled anchovy fillets,
to decorate

Strip the spinach, spinach beet or chard leaves from
the stalks by pulling them through a fork, and wash
until clean. Pack the washed leaves into a large
saucepan with the onion, parsley and tarragon, cover
with a lid and cook for 5–7 minutes, then drain
thoroughly. Roughly chop the cooked leaves and the
hard-boiled eggs.
  Bone the sardines and chop roughly. (If using
anchovies, drain them well, then chop.) Mix all these
ingredients in a blender or processor, then stir in the
cream, yoghurt or mayonnaise. Season to taste, then
spoon into one large dish or 6 individual dishes.
  Chill for 2–3 hours in the fridge, then decorate with
slices of hard-boiled egg and rolled anchovy fillets.
Serve with hot brown rolls, or thin wholemeal toast.
(Serves 6)

POTTED VENISON

*Beatrix Potter studied deer in their natural
state in Perthshire, while on the annual Potter
family summer holiday. There, potted venison would
no doubt have been regularly prepared and eaten. In those
days, potting was a way of preserving meat,
fish or game under a layer of butter. Today, a potted
dish provides an unusual starter, a simple lunch or the
perfect food for a picnic. This particular recipe was given to
me by Jean Butterworth, who established the reputation
of the famous White Moss House Hotel
at Rydal Water.*

150 g (5 oz/¾ cup) butter
2 large cloves of garlic, crushed
450 g (1 lb) cooked venison
75 g (3 oz/1 cup) fresh wholemeal breadcrumbs
150 g (5 oz) cream cheese
6 crushed juniper berries, or 1 teaspoon chopped
fresh lovage
Grated rind of 1 small orange
1 tablespoon brandy
Salt and freshly milled black pepper
Clarified butter, to cover
Bay leaves and juniper berries, to decorate

Melt the butter in a small pan and lightly cook the
garlic, then combine all the ingredients, except the
clarified butter and garnish, together in a food processor or blender. (Alternatively, mince the venison
finely, then thoroughly mix in all the other ingredients.) Season to taste, then pack into one suitable
large dish or 6–8 individual pots.

Cover with clarified butter and decorate with bay
leaves and juniper berries. Store in the fridge for 2–3
days before serving, to allow the flavours to mellow.

Serve with hot wholemeal toast and homemade
crab apple, quince or rowan jelly (see pages 157–160).
(Serves 6–8)

SMOKED HERDWICK MACON WITH RHUBARB AND ANGELICA MOUSSE

*Old Cumbrian mutton hams, or macons, would have been
well known in Beatrix Potter's time. Ashdown Smokers
near Waberthwaite in Cumbria, run by Harry and Kate
Fellows, are traditional curers and smokers famous for their
variety of fish and their smoked Herdwick macon which
they supply by mail order all over the country. After a dry
cure the muttons are smoked very slowly over gently
burning oak from Eskdale and aromatic juniper from
around Coniston. Harry and Kate sent me this unusual
recipe. The macon can, of course, be replaced by
any raw ham or Parma-style ham.*

900 g (2 lb) rhubarb, trimmed
1 tablespoon water
A few angelica leaves
125 g (4 oz/¾ cup) caster sugar
12 g (½ oz) gelatine or 2 × 6 g (¼ oz) envelopes
American gelatine
Juice of 1 lemon
150 ml (¼ pint/⅔ cup) double cream
2 large egg whites
12 slices smoked Herdwick macon
Fresh mint or angelica leaves, to garnish

Chop the rhubarb into even-sized chunks and place
in an ovenproof dish with the water, angelica and
sugar. Cook in a moderate oven until soft, then purée
in a blender or push through a sieve. Add 2 extra
finely-chopped angelica leaves to the purée.

Soften the gelatine in the lemon juice in a small
basin standing in a pan of hot water, then add to the
purée through a fine warmed sieve. Stir the gelatine
into the purée, then leave the mixture to cool.

Beat the cream until it stands in soft peaks, then
add it to the fruit mixture. Whisk the egg whites until
fairly stiff and fold them into the purée. Leave to set.

When the purée is set, spoon it on to the slices of
smoked macon and form them into rolls. Serve 2 rolls
for each person on individual plates and garnish
with mint or angelica leaves. (Serves 6)

Fish

Cornish buttered and creamed lobster 28

Crab-stuffed pancakes 29

Wild salmon with an orange and watercress sauce 30

Baked salmon fillets with elderflowers 31

West country cider-soused mackerel 32

Stuffed herrings with mustard sauce 33

Lakeland grilled trout with gooseberry sauce 35

Baked sea trout with cucumber and tarragon sauce 36

Haddock and prawn cobbler 37

Warm Esthwaite smoked trout salad 38

Moss Eccles nutty brown trout 39

Windermere char with a salmon mousseline 40

White moss pike and char soufflé 41

CORNISH BUTTERED AND CREAMED LOBSTER

---

*The Potter family used to leave London for
two or three weeks in April to stay in seaside hotels in
Lyme Regis, Minehead, Ilfracombe, Teignmouth, Sidmouth
or Falmouth. In 1892 they spent their Easter
holiday in Falmouth and Beatrix writes at length
in her journal about Cornwall. Living in Cornwall myself,
I was much amused by her observation of the
'locals': 'they are naive and unspoiled to an amusing
degree. Very friendly, kindly, cheerful, healthy – long lived
and the numerous old people very merry, which
speaks well for a race.' I would agree with her observation,
with the exception of 'naive'!
Lobster is still a popular Cornish dish with holidaymakers
out for a special treat. We 'locals' can't afford it!*

3 cooked lobsters, weighing 575–700 g
(1¼–1½ lb) each
Lemon juice
140 g (4 ½ oz/¾ cup) butter
40 g (1½ oz/½ cup) fresh breadcrumbs
½ teaspoon prepared English mustard
4 tablespoons (⅓ cup) brandy
75 ml (5 tablespoons/½ cup) double cream
or crème fraîche
Salt and freshly milled black pepper
Pinch of cayenne pepper
Lemon slices, to garnish
Sprigs of fresh dill or fennel, to garnish

Place the lobsters on a board, back upwards, and cut each one in half lengthways using a strong, sharp-pointed knife. Open out the two halves of each lobster and discard the gritty stomach sac from the head, the thin black thread of intestine that runs through the body and the spongy gills. Remove all the tail meat and reserve.

Twist off the claws and legs and, using a hammer or special lobster cracker, crack open the claws and remove the meat. Scrape the meat from the legs with a skewer.

Cut all the meat into chunks, then sprinkle with lemon juice. Remove and reserve the coral or roe, if present, and remove and reserve the soft pink flesh and the green creamy liver in the head, which are delicacies. Wash and scrub the empty shells and place in a slow oven (150°C, 300°F, gas mark 2) to warm.

Melt 40 g (1½ oz/¼ cup) of the butter in a small saucepan, add the breadcrumbs and cook gently until brown and crisp. Remove from the heat and leave on one side.

Melt the remaining butter in a large saucepan and add the mustard, then the lobster flesh. Heat through, stirring lightly, until evenly buttered. Heat the brandy in a ladle, then ignite and pour, still flaming, over the lobster meat. When the flames have died down, use a slotted spoon to transfer the lobster back into the warmed shells. Keep warm until ready to serve, reserving the delicious juices in the saucepan.

Pound the reserved pink flesh and liver together, then stir into the cooking juices. Add the cream and season to taste with a little salt, plenty of black pepper and the cayenne pepper. Bring to the boil and boil briefly until thick, then spoon the sauce over the lobster.

Sprinkle with the browned breadcrumbs (reheated if necessary) and garnish with the reserved coral, if available. Garnish with lemon slices and fresh dill or fennel. Serve with a green salad and wholemeal bread. (Serves 6)

*C*RAB-STUFFED PANCAKES

*While Beatrix Potter was away on her annual
holidays, she sent special picture letters to the young
children she knew. Her earliest known picture letter was
written when she was twenty-five and sent
to Noel Moore, the eldest son of her last governess.
The letter was written from the Falmouth Hotel
in Cornwall and tells Noel of a trip to St Mawes, where
Beatrix watched the local fishermen catching crabs in pots.
(See illustration below.)*

For the pancakes

75 g (3 oz/½ cup) plain flour
Pinch of salt
1 small egg, beaten
120 ml (4 fl oz/½ cup) milk
120 ml (4 fl oz/½ cup) water
75 g (3 oz/2 cups) finely chopped spinach
Sunflower oil, for frying

For the filling

250 g (8 oz) cooked, firm-fleshed white fish such as
cod, haddock or conger eel
125 g (4 oz) peeled prawns or lightly poached
scallops or queenies
50 g (2 oz) white crab meat
50 g (2 oz) brown crab meat
12 g (½ oz/1 tablespoon) butter
½ small onion, finely chopped
50 g (2 oz/⅓ cup) chopped mushrooms
½ teaspoon chopped fresh basil or a pinch of dried
1 tablespoon chopped fresh parsley
300 ml (½ pint/1¼ cups) white sauce
Salt and freshly milled black pepper
120 ml (4 fl oz/½ cup) dry white wine
2 (3 US) tablespoons double cream or yoghurt
50 g (2 oz/½ cup) grated Cheddar cheese (optional)
Chopped fresh parsley or basil, to garnish
Marigold petals, to garnish

To make the pancakes, sieve the flour and salt together into a basin. Mix the egg with the milk and water. Make a well in the centre of the dry ingredients and gradually add the liquid, whisking it into the flour until a smooth batter is formed.

Stir in the spinach, then leave the batter to stand for 1 hour in a cool place.

When ready to cook the pancakes, heat a little oil in a 20 cm (8 in) frying pan until it begins to smoke. Pour in about 4 tablespoons (¼ cup) of the batter and cook over a high heat for 1–2 minutes until the bottom bubbles, then loosen and turn over to cook the other side. Slide the pancake on to a warm plate and continue in the same way with the rest of the batter. Stack the pancakes on top of each other between sheets of greaseproof paper or foil and keep warm on a low heat in the oven. (The pancakes can be made in advance and stored in the fridge for 4 days, or in the freezer for a month.)

Pre-heat the oven to 180°C (350°F, gas mark 4).

For the filling, mix all the fish together (if using scallops, chop them up roughly). Melt the butter in a small saucepan and cook the onion until soft and transparent. Add the mushrooms and cook for a few minutes, then add to the fish mixture with the basil and parsley. Mix in a little white sauce to bind the mixture together and season to taste. Divide the filling between the pancakes and roll up. Place the pancakes in a lightly buttered ovenproof dish.

Mix the remaining white sauce with the wine and cream or yoghurt and heat up gently. Pour over the filled pancakes and sprinkle with cheese, if using. Bake in the centre of a moderate oven for about 20 minutes, or until heated through, then flash under a hot grill for a few minutes until the top is bubbling and brown.

Serve immediately, garnished with parsley or basil and marigold petals. Accompany with a mixed or green salad. (Serves 6)

Pictured right, wild salmon with orange and watercress sauce

$\mathcal{W}$ILD SALMON WITH AN ORANGE AND WATERCRESS SAUCE

From the time Beatrix was five until she was fifteen, she spent every summer in Perthshire at Dalguise House, an elegant mansion overlooking the river Tay near Dunkeld. Her father, Rupert Potter, invited his friends from London to hunt and fish at Dalguise: Millais, the painter, John Bright, the politician, and William Gaskell, a great favourite with young Beatrix. The Tay is probably Scotland's most famous salmon river and there were many successful fishing expeditions. Beatrix reports in her journal on 27 October, 1884, 'Been splendid salmon fishing in the Tay this year. Mr Millais caught one 44 lb'! What superb dinners the visitors must have enjoyed at Dalguise. Wild salmon tastes wonderful but is difficult to buy these days. The following recipe can use either wild or farmed salmon.

6 salmon steaks, about 2.5 cm (1 in) thick
50 g (2 oz/¼ cup) butter, melted
Salt and freshly milled black pepper
Watercress, to garnish
Orange slices, to garnish

For the sauce

1 small bunch of watercress
300 ml (½ pint/1¼ cups) strong fish stock
Juice of 1 orange
1 teaspoon cornflour
150 ml (¼ pint/⅔ cup) single cream
Salt and freshly milled black pepper

Cut 6 rectangles of greaseproof paper, large enough to wrap up each salmon steak. Brush well with melted butter and place a salmon steak in the centre

30

of each rectangle. Season the fish on both sides with salt and pepper, then wrap up carefully so that none of the juices can escape during cooking. Steam over simmering water for about 10–15 minutes, or until just cooked. Unwrap the parcels and transfer the steaks to a warm serving dish.

While the fish is cooking, the orange and watercress sauce can be made. Wash and dry the watercress and pick all the leaves. Purée them in a blender or processor with the fish stock, then add orange juice to taste. Mix the cornflour with the cream and add to the watercress mixture. Blend or process, then transfer to a saucepan. Stir the sauce over a low heat until it thickens a little, then season to taste with salt and pepper.

Arrange the salmon steaks on plates, garnished with more watercress and orange slices, and serve the sauce separately. (Serves 6)

ℬAKED SALMON FILLETS WITH ELDERFLOWERS

In 1892 Rupert Potter decided to take the family back to Scotland for their summer holiday, after a break of several summers spent in the Lake District. Their beloved Dalguise House was no longer available, so he rented Heath Park in Birnam. The house was not big enough to accommodate visitors, so the Potters followed their own amusements. Rupert and Beatrix's brother Bertram spent a great deal of time fishing both the Braan and the Tay for salmon. Heath Park was situated 'a convenient remove' from Birnam station and in her journal, Beatrix describes how she 'looked over the hedge at many salmon packed in straw [to] go off by the mail. One weighed 45 lb.'

6 salmon fillets
Freshly milled sea salt and black pepper
6 elderflower heads
150 ml (¼ pint/⅔ cup) dry white wine
Sprigs of fresh chervil or parsley, to garnish
Tiny sprigs of elderflowers, to garnish

For the sauce

75 g (3 oz/6 US tablespoons) butter
2 shallots, finely sliced
400 ml (13 fl oz/1⅔ cups) fish stock
100 ml (3 fl oz/⅓ cup) double cream or crème fraîche
Freshly milled sea salt and black pepper

Pre-heat the oven to 180°C (350°F, gas mark 4).

Season the salmon well and place in a shallow buttered ovenproof dish. Check that the elderflower heads are clean and insect-free and remove most of the thicker stalks. Tuck them between the salmon fillets and pour in the wine. Cover tightly with foil and bake in a moderate oven for about 20 minutes, or until the fish is just cooked. Strain off 100 ml (3 fl oz/⅓ cup) of the cooking liquor for the sauce, then cover again and keep warm.

To make the sauce, heat 12 g (½ oz/1 tablespoon) of the butter in a pan and cook the shallots until soft. Add the cooking liquor and boil until almost completely reduced. Add the fish stock and bring to the boil again. Continue boiling until reduced by about three-quarters, then stir in the cream. Boil until reduced by about one-third then, using a balloon whisk, whisk in the remaining butter a little at a time. Taste and adjust the seasoning as necessary.

To serve, place a salmon fillet on each plate, discarding the elderflowers, and spoon a little of the sauce around. Garnish with sprigs of herb and tiny clusters of elderflowers. (Serves 6)

𝒲EST COUNTRY CIDER-SOUSED MACKEREL

On holiday in Falmouth in 1892, Beatrix watched the fishermen with great interest, noting 'an odoriferous person who hawked mackerels'.

6 very fresh mackerel, filleted
10 black peppercorns
6 whole cloves
4 bay leaves
4 sprigs of fresh thyme
2 blades of mace
Pinch of ground allspice
1 medium onion, finely sliced
150 ml (¼ pint/⅔ cup) cider vinegar
Enough dry cider to cover
Freshly milled sea salt
150 ml (¼ pint/⅔ cup) thick natural yoghurt
Sprigs of watercress and apple slices, to garnish

Pre-heat the oven to 180°C (350°F, gas mark 4).

Arrange the fish in a lightly greased deep oven-proof dish. Bruise the peppercorns and cloves a little with a pestle and mortar and sprinkle over the fish. Scatter the bay leaves over and tuck in the thyme. Add the mace and allspice, then arrange the onion slices over the fish. Pour over the cider vinegar and enough dry cider barely to cover. Season generously with salt, cover loosely with foil and bake in a moderate oven for about 30 minutes.

Carefully lift out the fish, discarding any of the flavouring ingredients. Place in a clean dish and strain over the cider mixture. Cool, then chill in the fridge until needed. (Mackerel prepared in this way will keep for 1 week, providing they remain immersed in the liquid.)

To serve, carefully lift out the fillets with a fish slice and arrange on a serving dish. Spoon over the yoghurt and garnish with a few sprigs of watercress and apple slices. Accompany with crusty wholemeal or soda bread and a green salad with hard-boiled eggs for a delicious summer lunch. (Serves 6)

*S*TUFFED HERRINGS WITH MUSTARD SAUCE

*Beatrix Potter wrote in her journal of a 'very
enjoyable expedition' to Berwick with her father
on a 'gloriously cloudless day' in September, 1894, to
take photographs of the boats. She 'waited about a long
time among the herrings watching a boat unload. They had
. . . an immense quantity in appearance, as
they shovelled them into a basket. Eight shillings for
two barrels, a poor price, according to a somewhat morosely
incommunicative mother with dinner-basket.'
Herrings are rich in a group of essential
polyunsaturated fatty acids which are found
only in oily fish and are good for the heart. Including
oily fish in your diet once or twice a week therefore makes
good sense. In this recipe, the roes are used
in a stuffing for the fish; sharp mustard sauce makes a
good accompaniment. Mackerel, pilchards or sardines can
be cooked in the same way.*

6 medium herrings with soft roes, cleaned
450 ml (¾ pint/scant 2 cups) milk
90 g (3½ oz/½ cup) butter
3 shallots or 1 small onion, finely chopped
40 g (1½ oz/½ cup) fresh breadcrumbs
Grated rind of ½ lemon
1 tablespoon lemon juice
1 heaped tablespoon chopped fresh parsley and
chives, mixed together
1 tablespoon chopped fresh tarragon, dill or chervil
or 1 teaspoon dried
Salt and freshly milled black pepper
3 tablespoons (¼ cup) plain flour
Prepared Cumberland or English mustard
1½ teaspoons white wine vinegar
6 lemon wedges, to garnish
Sprigs of fresh parsley, chervil or dill, to garnish

Pre-heat the oven to 180°C (350°F, gas mark 4).

Cut the heads, tails and fins off the fish, then lay
them flat on a board, skin-side up. Press firmly along
the centre of the fish to loosen the backbone, then
turn the fish over. Starting at the head, ease away the
backbone with the tip of a knife, removing as many
of the small bones as possible at the same time.

Put the roes in a small pan with the milk and
simmer gently for 1–2 minutes, then drain, reserving
the milk. Chop the roes finely.

Melt just over half the butter in a small pan and
cook the shallots or onion very gently until transpar-
e'nt and golden. Mix together the breadcrumbs,
lemon rind and juice, herbs and cooked roes, then
stir in the cooked onion. Season to taste, then spread
on the open herrings. Fold them over to enclose the
stuffing.

Arrange the fish in a well-buttered baking dish
and bake for 20–30 minutes, or until tender.

Meanwhile, to make the sauce, melt the remaining
butter in a pan. Stir in the flour and cook for a few
minutes. Gradually stir in the reserved milk, then
heat gently, stirring frequently, until the sauce is
thick and smooth. Bring to the boil and simmer for
about 5 minutes.

Just before serving, stir mustard to taste into the
sauce, starting with 1 teaspoon, and add the vinegar.
Season well with salt and pepper. (Don't bring the
sauce to the boil again or the taste of the mustard will
be spoiled.)

Place the herrings on a warmed serving dish and
pour over the sauce. Garnish with lemon wedges and
sprigs of fresh herb. Serve with a salad or green
vegetable. (Serves 6)

Illustration from The Tale of Little Pig Robinson

*L*AKELAND GRILLED TROUT WITH GOOSEBERRY SAUCE

Beatrix had been accustomed from childhood to go fishing for trout and salmon with her brother, Bertram, on their country holidays in Scotland and the Lake District. Her letters from those earlier days often refer to fishing expeditions with Bertram.

In her later life trout and salmon were also a fairly frequent luxury, as her husband Willie Heelis was a keen dry-fly fisherman. In a letter of July, 1922 to Sylvie Heelis, Beatrix tells her, 'Uncle Willie has gone out fishing – or poaching; rather an odd performance, occasionally resulting in 1 lb trouts.' Perhaps Beatrix and Willie enjoyed grilled trout with gooseberry sauce; they grew gooseberries in the garden and it is a very traditional combination. The sauce is also good with duck, pork, lamb and veal.

Mackerel or herrings may be used instead of trout for this recipe, which is based on one given to me by Eleanor Quinlan. Eleanor and her husband Richard run the Mill Hotel, a former seventeenth century mill cottage in Mungrisdale excelling in food full of flavour and honest goodness.

6 very fresh good-sized trout
125 g (4 oz/½ cup) butter, melted
Freshly milled black pepper

For the sauce

450 g (1 lb) fresh or frozen gooseberries
5 tablespoons (½ cup) dry white wine
1 standard (medium) egg
Salt and freshly milled black pepper
Ground ginger or freshly grated nutmeg

Clean the fish, leaving the heads and tails intact, but removing the gills. Wipe the skin well with a damp cloth, but do not wash. Line a baking tray or grill pan with buttered foil and place the trout on the foil. Slash the fish two or three times diagonally across the body on both sides and brush generously with melted butter. Season well with black pepper.

To make the sauce, wash and top and tail the gooseberries. Place them in a pan with the wine and simmer gently until the fruit is very tender. Remove from the heat and beat in the egg with a wooden spoon. Season with salt, pepper and ginger or nutmeg. Keep warm while you cook the trout.

Place the fish under a hot grill and cook for about 5 minutes on each side, depending on the size, or until the skin is just starting to brown.

Serve at once with the sauce spooned over the trout.

Variations

A little honey may be added to the sauce if you find it too tart, but it should be on the sharp side. One tablespoon chopped fresh fennel is a good addition and 1 tablespoon yoghurt, cream or fromage frais can also be stirred in. (Serves 6)

Lakeland grilled trout with gooseberry sauce, photographed in the grounds of the Mill Hotel, Mungrisdale

BAKED SEA TROUT WITH CUCUMBER AND TARRAGON SAUCE

*Beatrix Potter wrote in her journal of a trip
to Berwick on 28 August, 1894, with her brother
Bertram, while they were on their annual family holiday
in Perthshire. They spent a day at the seaside, watching the
salmon fishermen and the boats 'with their
heavy, brown sails' and hunting on the beach
for fossils and wild flowers. Beatrix finished the trip
by buying 'a great salmon trout out of the heap at the
fishmonger's, and not being wise or experienced in marketing
was seized with apprehensions, but it proved excellent.'
A whole sea or salmon trout makes a wonderful
dinner-party dish and is easy to cook. The flavour is
more delicate than salmon, so a fresh-tasting cucumber
sauce is an ideal accompaniment.*

1.5 kg (3–3½ lb) sea trout, cleaned
50 g (2 oz/¼ cup) butter, melted
Freshly milled sea salt and black pepper
4 tablespoons (⅓ cup) dry white wine
Lemon or lime slices, to garnish
Sprigs of fresh tarragon or chervil and chive flowers,
to garnish

For the sauce

1 firm medium cucumber (2 American cucumbers)
75 g (3 oz/6 US tablespoons) butter
4 tablespoons (⅓ cup) double cream, yoghurt or
crème fraîche
½ teaspoon lemon juice, if using cream
Freshly milled sea salt and white pepper
1 teaspoon chopped fresh tarragon

Pre-heat the oven to 180°C (350°F, gas mark 4).

Leave the head and tail of the fish intact, but cut off the gills. Wipe with a damp cloth, rather than washing.

Place the fish in the centre of a large piece of buttered foil. Brush generously with the melted butter on both sides and sprinkle with salt and pepper inside and out. Pour over the wine, then wrap up the fish in the foil to make a parcel. Place on a baking tray and bake in a moderate oven for about 50 minutes, or until the fish is tender. (Test with a skewer in the thickest part.)

Meanwhile, make the sauce. Wipe the cucumber and chop it coarsely, then melt the butter over a low heat and add the cucumber. Cook for a few minutes until heated through, then cool. Purée in a blender or processor with the cream or yoghurt. Add the lemon juice if you have used cream, then season with salt and pepper to taste, and return the purée to the pan. The sauce may be completed to this point several hours ahead, then covered and refrigerated until needed.

Just before serving, reheat the sauce gently, stirring in the tarragon. Serve separately in a warmed jug. When the fish is cooked, unwrap it and transfer carefully to a warmed serving dish. Serve immediately as it is, or remove the skin first. Garnish with slices of lemon or lime, sprigs of fresh herb and chive flowers.

Eat the fish with new potatoes or crusty wholemeal bread, a green vegetable or salad. (Serves 6)

Variation

Chopped dill, fennel or basil may be added to the sauce instead of tarragon.

*H*ADDOCK AND PRAWN COBBLER

Memories of several of Beatrix Potter's seaside holidays are included in her story The Tale of Little Pig Robinson. *Many of the town and harbour scenes are based on places in Devon and Dorset, while the old fishermen's huts are still to be seen, just as Beatrix drew them, on the shore at Hastings in Sussex. The Potter family must frequently have enjoyed fresh fish straight from the boats while they were on holiday.*
In this family dish, use a mixture of fresh and naturally smoked haddock or cod.

450 g (1 lb) haddock fillet
250 g (8 oz) naturally smoked haddock (without colouring)
600 ml (1 pint/2½ cups) milk
125 g (4 oz/½ cup) butter
Salt and freshly milled black pepper
50 g (2 oz/⅓ cup) plain flour
125 g (4 oz) peeled prawns
2 hard-boiled eggs, chopped
1 tablespoon capers
½ small red pepper, finely chopped
3 tablespoons (¼ cup) chopped fresh parsley
Juice of ½ a lemon

For the topping

125 g (4 oz/¾ cup) self-raising white flour
125 g (4 oz/¾ cup) self-raising wholemeal flour
or plain wholemeal flour sifted with
1 teaspoon baking powder
Pinch of salt
50 g (2 oz/¼ cup) butter
½ tablespoon chopped fresh parsley
1½ teaspoons chopped fresh thyme or ½ teaspoon dried
2 teaspoons dry mustard
75 g (3 oz/¾ cup) grated mature Cheddar cheese
About 150 ml (¼ pint/⅔ cup) milk or natural yoghurt
Extra milk, for glazing
Sprigs of fresh parsley, to garnish

Pre-heat the oven to 200°C (400°F, gas mark 6).

Place the fresh and smoked haddock in a buttered ovenproof dish and pour over half the milk. Dot with 25 g (1 oz/2 tablespoons) of the butter and season well. Bake in a moderate oven for 15–20 minutes, or until tender. Drain off and reserve the cooking liquor.

Remove the skin from the fish when cool and flake the flesh into fairly large pieces; set aside. Melt the remaining butter in a pan, then stir in the flour. Cook for 2 minutes, then remove from the heat and gradually stir in the reserved cooking liquor. Put back on the heat and slowly add the remaining milk. Season with salt and pepper to taste.

Mix the fish into this white sauce, with the prawns, hard-boiled eggs, capers, red pepper and parsley. Stir in the lemon juice and taste. Adjust seasoning as necessary, then transfer the mixture into a well-buttered 1.5-litre (2½-pint/1½-quart US) deep ovenproof dish.

To make the topping, sieve both flours and salt into a mixing bowl and rub in the butter. Stir in the herbs, mustard and cheese, then mix with enough milk or yoghurt to make a soft dough. Knead lightly on a floured surface and roll or pat out into a circle large enough to cover the top of the ovenproof dish. Cut the dough into quarters, and then again to make 8 triangles. Place them over the fish mixture, so that the points meet in the centre.

Brush with milk and bake in a hot oven, 220°C (425°F, gas mark 7), for about 25 minutes, or until the pastry topping is golden brown and well-risen. Garnish with sprigs of parsley and serve immediately with a green vegetable or a green salad for lunch or supper. (Serves 6)

WARM ESTHWAITE SMOKED TROUT SALAD

During their Lake District holiday in 1896, the Potter family kept a boat on Esthwaite Water and Beatrix describes in a letter how much she enjoyed rowing alone on the lake. Esthwaite was to remain her favourite lake all her life. She sketched and painted it many times; the view from the wood in The Tale of Jemima Puddle-Duck *shows Esthwaite, and Mr. Jeremy Fisher's adventures are thought by some to have taken place on this lake. Esthwaite is virtually unchanged today, but there is now a small trout farm on the Hawkshead side of the lake where you can buy freshly caught and smoked trout. Nigel Woodhouse, who runs the farm, gave me this recipe.*
The photograph above shows Esthwaite trout on the landing-stage of the farm.

1 crisp lettuce
½ cucumber (1 American cucumber)
2 bunches radishes
125 g (4 oz) button mushrooms
2 (3 US) tablespoons olive oil
6 smoked trout, flaked
A few butter-fried wholemeal bread croutons
About 12 black olives

For the dressing

5 tablespoons (½ cup) light olive or sunflower oil
2½ (3 US) tablespoons orange juice
3 teaspoons white wine vinegar
½ teaspoon clear honey
½ teaspoon Dijon mustard
Freshly milled sea salt and black pepper
1 teaspoon grated orange rind
½ teaspoon horseradish cream

38

To prepare the salad, wash and dry the lettuce, slice the cucumber (including the skin), wash, trim and slice the radishes and wipe and slice the mushrooms. Arrange the salad ingredients on 6 separate plates.

To make the dressing, put all the ingredients in a small screw-topped jar and shake together very thoroughly. Taste and adjust seasoning as you like.

Heat 2 tablespoons olive oil in a heavy frying pan until smoking, add the flaked trout and cook for 1 minute until heated through, turning gently. Sprinkle the prepared salads with a few warm croutons, then divide the trout between the 6 plates. Drizzle over the dressing and decorate with black olives.

Serve at once with new potatoes. (Serves 6)

MOSS ECCLES NUTTY BROWN TROUT

Moss Eccles Tarn is a peaceful little lake above the village of Near Sawrey, in the Lake District. Beatrix bought part of the tarn along with Castle Cottage, her married home, and planted waterlilies and stocked it with brown trout. Her husband Willie would fish there and Beatrix would sit in the boat with him, maybe deciding on the method of cooking whatever he caught! Their boat was recovered from the bed of the tarn in 1976 and is now one of many fascinating exhibits at the Bowness Steamboat Museum.

Moss Eccles was given by Beatrix to the National Trust, and is still a peaceful and magical place today. When I arrived in Sawrey for the first time, I retraced Beatrix and Willie's footsteps to the tarn and relaxed there in the evening light after my long journey from Cornwall. As a perfect ending to the day, freshly caught Moss Eccles brown trout was on the menu for dinner, as it must have been many times at Castle Cottage.

Brown or rainbow trout may be used for this recipe, which is very easy, but so good. For a special occasion, serve the fish for breakfast with home-cured smoked bacon, hot wholemeal toast and farm butter.

350 g (12 oz/2¾ cups) shelled hazelnuts
6 very fresh medium trout
Freshly milled black pepper
Lemon juice
A little flour
Freshly milled sea salt
3 large eggs
1 tablespoon milk
175 g (6 oz/¾ cup) clarified butter
12 grapefruit or lime segments, to garnish
Watercress, to garnish

Grill or roast the hazelnuts until their skins can be rubbed off using a tea towel; then chop them. Clean the fish, leaving the heads and tails intact but removing the gills. Then wipe the trout lightly with a damp cloth, rather than washing. Rub the skins gently with plenty of black pepper and sprinkle with lemon juice. Dust very lightly with flour and then season with a little salt.

Beat the eggs with the milk, then dip the trout in this mixture. Finally, roll the fish in the chopped hazelnuts.

Melt the clarified butter in a large heavy pan and fry the fish over a moderate heat for about 5 minutes on each side, lightly pressing the fish down into the pan so that the skin crisps to a delicious golden brown. The trout are cooked if the flesh gives when pressed gently in the thickest part with the fingertips.

Remove the trout to a hot serving dish and pour over the pan juices. Serve immediately, garnished with grapefruit or lime segments and sprigs of watercress. Eat with plenty of crusty homemade bread. (Serves 6)

WINDERMERE CHAR WITH A SALMON MOUSSELINE

The char is the rarest Lakeland fish; eating fresh char is one of the perks of living there. It is the size of a small trout, but silver, scarlet and olive green in colour. The flesh is pinkish – rather like a salmon trout, but more delicate in flavour. The char is confined to very deep lakes and is most common in Windermere, where it is a local delicacy.

In the seventeenth, eighteenth and nineteenth centuries, char pie and potted char were so fashionable that there was a danger of the species being overfished. The Potter family probably ate potted char with toast for breakfast while on holiday in Windermere.

Eleanor Quinlan often uses the local Windermere char for the recipe with gooseberry sauce described on page 35. Jean Butterworth, who is very knowledgeable about traditional Lakeland food and gave me this recipe, suggests that trout be used if char is not available.

350 g (12 oz) salmon or sole fillet
200 ml (8 fl oz/1 cup) double cream
2 egg whites
Large pinch of ground coriander
Large pinch of ground mace or nutmeg
Freshly milled sea salt and white pepper
6 char or small trout, cleaned
Sprigs of watercress, to garnish

For the sauce

2 (3 US) tablespoons white wine vinegar
3 (4 US) tablespoons water
1 slice of onion
Blade of mace
½ a small bayleaf
6 black peppercorns, lightly crushed
1 tablespoon water
Salt and freshly milled black pepper
3 egg yolks
175 g (6 oz/¾ cup) unsalted butter
Grated rind of 1 orange
Orange juice to taste

To make the mousseline, skin the salmon or sole, remove any bones, and cut into chunks. Put the fish chunks, the blender goblet or processor bowl and the cream into the freezer for about 20 minutes to chill well. Process the chilled fish to the finest possible paste, then add the egg whites one by one with the motor running. Add the coriander and mace or nutmeg, then check to see that the fish mixture is still very cold. (Put back in the freezer for another 10 minutes if necessary.) When cold, add the cream very slowly, again with the motor running. Season to taste with pepper and salt.

Pre-heat the oven to 180°C (350°F, gas mark 4).

Cut off the heads, tails and fins of the char or trout and open out on a board. Spread flat, skin-side up, then press along the centre back of the fish to loosen the backbone. Turn over and then, starting at the head, ease away the backbone with a sharp knife, removing as many small bones as possible also.

Pipe or spoon the mousseline into the prepared char or trout and fold over. Arrange the fish on a baking tray covered with buttered foil, then cover with more buttered foil and bake in the centre of the oven for about 20 minutes or until cooked, depending on the size of the fish. (The flesh should give easily when pressed gently with the fingertips.)

Prepare the sauce while the fish is cooking. Place the vinegar, water, onion, mace, bay leaf and peppercorns in a small pan. Simmer gently until the mixture is reduced to about 1 tablespoon, then strain into a bowl. Add a further tablespoon of water and a little salt and pepper. Whisk in the egg yolks.

Set the bowl over a pan of barely simmering water and whisk in 12 g (½ oz/1 tablespoon) of the butter, whisking until it has melted. Continue adding the butter, cut into small pieces, allowing each piece to melt completely before adding the next.

When all the butter has been added, continue to whisk the sauce and cook gently for a further few minutes until thick. Then remove the bowl from the pan of water and add the orange rind and orange juice. Taste and correct the seasoning if necessary.

Arrange the fish on a serving dish and garnish with watercress. Serve the sauce separately. (Serves 6)

WHITE MOSS PIKE AND CHAR SOUFFLÉ

The pike caught in Rydal Water and Grasmere is cleaner and has a less muddy flavour than river pike; the water comes straight down off the fells and consequently is very clean. You can actually see the bottom in places. Char is not fished commercially, as it lives in deep water and is difficult to catch, but occasionally it appears on the fishmonger's slab. Most of the char caught ends up at hotels and restaurants, particularly in April and May when the fish comes to spawn in shallower water.

The recipe for a delectable soufflé combining these two locally caught fish comes from Peter Dixon who, with his wife Sue, has been running the famous White Moss House Hotel at Rydal Water for ten years. They took over from the Butterworths, Sue's parents, and have continued to gain top awards in all the restaurant guides. White Moss once belonged to Wordsworth and is a typical Lakeland house, so traditional home-cooked food suits the place well. Soufflés are a particular speciality and Peter has become an expert. His most important tip is to make sure that the consistency of the 'sauce' is the same as the whisked egg whites. If it is too thick, let it down with a little warm water. Cooking the soufflé in a bain marie brings it up beautifully and it will stay up!

75 g (3 oz) pike or perch
75 g (3 oz) char or salmon
Dry white wine, to cover
Freshly milled sea salt and black pepper
50 g (2 oz/¼ cup) butter
50 g (2 oz/⅓ cup) strong plain flour
300 ml (½ pint/1¼ cups) hot milk (or milk mixed with stock made from pike bones)
Pinch of cayenne pepper
Pinch of freshly grated nutmeg
4 egg yolks
75 g (3 oz/¾ cup) grated cheese (Double Gloucester gives a good colour)
1 tablespoon chopped fresh fennel, dill or basil or 1 teaspoon dried
5 egg whites
Pinch of cream of tartar

Place the fish in a shallow pan and pour over enough white wine barely to cover. Season lightly with salt and pepper. Poach very gently for a few minutes until just cooked, then remove the fish, discard the skin and bones and flake the flesh.

Melt the butter in a large saucepan and stir in the flour with a wooden spoon. Cook for about 2 minutes until foaming, but not brown, then remove from the heat. When the bubbling has stopped, gradually beat in the hot milk, followed by some more salt and pepper and the cayenne and nutmeg. Return to the heat and cook for 1–2 minutes, stirring continuously until smooth. Remove from the heat again and leave to cool slightly. Beat in the egg yolks, one at a time. (The mixture can be prepared up to this point earlier in the day if you wish, but bring back to a tepid temperature before you start the next stage.)

Pre-heat the oven to 190°C (375°F, gas mark 5).

Stir the fish into this sauce with the cheese and the herbs until well mixed. Then whisk the egg whites in a large mixing bowl with a pinch of salt and cream of tartar until stiff. Stir 1 large spoonful of egg white into the sauce to lighten its texture, then lightly fold in the rest, taking care not to overmix.

Pour the mixture gently into a generously buttered 1.5 litre (2½ pint/1½ US quart) soufflé dish. Smooth the surface and mark the top in a criss-cross pattern with a skewer. Stand the soufflé dish in a deep roasting tin half-filled with hot water and cook in the centre of the oven for 5 minutes, then reduce to moderate, 180°C (350°F, gas mark 4), for a further 40 minutes. The soufflé should be nicely risen, and golden brown on top. Serve with a crisp green salad for lunch or supper. (Serves 6)

Variation

INDIVIDUAL PIKE AND CHAR SOUFFLÉS

Make as before but place the mixture in individual buttered ramekins. Cook in a roasting tin containing hot water half-way up the ramekins, for 5 minutes at 190°C (375°F, gas mark 5), then about 30 minutes at 180°C (350°F, gas mark 4).

Meat

ℐATIE POT

*Never a hunt or a supper or 'owt' goes by without a good
tatie pot in Lakeland and everyone has their own recipe.
The traditional version, which Beatrix and Willie must
have eaten many times at local events, uses plenty of good
Herdwick mutton, black pudding and potatoes – originally
more potatoes and less meat, giving the dish its name. Black
pudding made from pig's blood and oatmeal is a great
delicacy in the North and, in a good tatie pot, melts during
cooking to give a deliciously dark rich gravy. This
particular recipe uses lamb, as mutton is often hard to get
hold of, and is best started a day ahead. It is a most
succulent hot-pot, served with pickled red cabbage and
usually northern mashed turnips (swede).*

1.6 kg (3½ lb) best end and middle neck of lamb,
in chops
Seasoned flour
3 large onions, finely sliced
4 large carrots, thickly sliced
1 large turnip or swede, roughly chopped
Lamb stock or water, to cover
3 or 4 sprigs of fresh mint
1 bay leaf
Salt and freshly milled black pepper
450 g (1 lb) black pudding, thickly sliced
900 g (2 lb) potatoes, thinly sliced

Pre-heat the oven to 140°C (275°F, gas mark 1).

Trim the fat and skin from the meat and cut up the
fat finely. Melt it in a large frying pan. Roll the
trimmed chops in seasoned flour, then brown all
over in the fat. Remove with a slotted spoon and
arrange in a large, shallow ovenproof dish. Fry the
onions, adding extra dripping if necessary, until soft.
Add the carrots and turnip and fry for a few minutes
more.

Transfer the vegetables to the ovenproof dish and
pour over enough stock or water to cover. Add the
mint and bay leaf and season well. Cover with a lid
or foil and cook in a very slow oven for 4–5 hours, or
until the meat falls off the bone easily. Strain off the
cooking liquor and leave until cold, preferably overnight.

The next day, pre-heat the oven to 190°C (375°F,
gas mark 5).

Bone the meat and cut into bite-sized chunks.
Discard the mint and bay leaf. Arrange back in the
cleaned ovenproof dish with the vegetables and
cover with slices of black pudding. Remove and
reserve the fat from the cold stock, then boil the stock
up in a pan. Taste and adjust the seasoning as
necessary, and pour over the meat, to cover. Arrange
overlapping slices of potato over the top and dot with
the reserved lamb fat. Season the potato, then cover
with the lid or foil and cook in a fairly hot oven for
about 1 hour, removing the lid or foil after 30
minutes to crisp and brown the potatoes at the edges.
(Brown under the grill for a few minutes if you wish.)

Serve hot with mashed turnips (swede), pickled
onions and pickled red cabbage (see page 163).
(Serves 6)

Beatrix Potter's Lakeland sheep, illustrated in The Fairy Caravan

DEVONSHIRE SQUAB PIE

After the First World War, a bakery was started in Beatrix Potter's village, Near Sawrey, at Anvil Cottage. Fridays were red-letter days, for Friday was Meat-Pie Day in Near Sawrey. The pies were so much in demand that villagers, including Beatrix Potter, queued to buy them. Mollie Green, who still serves teas in Anvil Cottage, remembers her mother simmering meat bones on the hob for hours and hours to make jelly stock for the pastry-covered pork pies. Devonshire squab pie is not made from pork, or young pigeons, but lamb. It is a popular pie in many parts of the West Country.

For the pastry

175 g (6 oz/1¼ cups) self-raising white flour
175 g (6 oz/1¼ cups) plain wholemeal flour
Large pinch of salt
75 g (3 oz/6 US tablespoons) butter or margarine
75 g (3 oz/6 US tablespoons) lard
Ice-cold water, to mix
Beaten egg and milk, to glaze

For the filling

900 g (2 lb) boned leg or shoulder of lamb
575 g (1¼ lb) onions, finely sliced
2 large cooking apples
Large pinch of ground mace
Large pinch of freshly grated nutmeg
1 tablespoon mixed chopped fresh mint, basil and rosemary or 1 teaspoon dried
Salt and freshly milled black pepper
225 ml (7½ fl oz/scant 1 cup) lamb or vegetable stock
150 ml (¼ pint/⅔ cup) double cream or crème fraîche

First make the pastry. Sieve the flours and salt together into a mixing bowl. Cut the fats into the flour with a palette knife, then rub in with your fingertips until the mixture resembles breadcrumbs. Add enough ice-cold water to make a stiff dough and knead lightly until smooth. Place in a polythene bag and leave in the fridge for at least 30 minutes while you prepare the filling.

Pre-heat the oven to 200°C (400°F, gas mark 6), then 180°C (350°F, gas mark 4).

Cut the meat into 2.5-cm (1-in) chunks and place half in the bottom of a 1-litre (2-pint/5-cup) pie-dish. Arrange half the onion slices over the top. Peel, core and slice the apples and add half to the pie. Sprinkle with the mace, nutmeg and half the herbs, then season well. Repeat the layers, then pour over the stock.

Roll out the prepared pastry to fit the pie-dish and use to cover the filling, moistening the edges of the pastry to seal. Use pastry trimmings to decorate the pie and make a hole in the top to let out the steam during cooking. Brush with beaten egg and milk and bake in a fairly hot oven for 20 minutes. Reduce the temperature to 180°C (350°F, gas mark 4) and cook for a further 1¼–1½ hours, covering the pastry with foil if it is browning too quickly.

Remove from the oven and gently lift up part of the pastry lid. Stir in the cream and adjust the seasoning as necessary. Replace the portion of pastry and reheat for a few minutes before serving.

Eat hot with boiled or mashed potatoes, a crisp green vegetable and hot beetroot or red cabbage. (Serves 6)

STUFFED LOIN OF WESTMORLAND LAMB

_____

Beatrix Potter bought her first property in 1905, a working farm called Hill Top in the Lake District village of Near Sawrey. The farm manager, John Cannon, purchased sixteen ewes the year after and the farm started to expand quite quickly. Beatrix had always noticed sheep, commenting throughout her journal on the various species, wherever she found them: Southdown sheep at Rue, Highland sheep at Birnam, the 'great Ram Sale' of Border Leicesters at Kelso in 1894, the ugly cross-breds, Dorset sheep and Cheviots. Now she had to look at them with a farmer's eye: 'I have been photographing this morning, photographing the lambs before they depart – Oh, shocking! It does not do to be sentimental on a farm. I am going to have some lambskin hearthrugs.'
Traditional Lakeland ingredients are used in this recipe, which is based on one from the Lakeside Hotel on Windermere. Redcurrant, damson, sloe, or rowan jelly may be used instead of blackcurrant – a favourite with the Heelises.

2 kg (4 lb) loin of lamb, boned flat (reserve bones for stock)
450 g (1 lb) Cumberland sausagemeat, or good quality pork sausagemeat
25 g (1 oz/¼ cup) fresh mint leaves
Freshly milled sea salt and black pepper
3 sprigs of fresh rosemary
Sprigs of fresh mint, to garnish

For the gravy

1 medium onion, finely sliced
1 teaspoon wholemeal flour
300 ml (½ pint/1¼ cups) strong lamb stock, made from the lamb bones
About 1 tablespoon blackcurrant jelly (see page 156)
Salt and freshly milled black pepper
About 1 tablespoon red wine

Pre-heat the oven to 180°C (350°F, gas mark 4).

If the lamb is rolled and tied, undo it and lay out flat. Remove the skin and any excess fat, then score the upper surface lightly with a sharp knife. Mix the sausagemeat and mint leaves together and spoon in a line down the middle of the inside of the lamb. Roll up lengthways to form a swiss-roll shape and tie up securely with string at regular intervals. Weigh the prepared joint to calculate the cooking time, then place in a roasting tin. Sprinkle with salt and pepper and tuck the rosemary under the string. Roast in the pre-heated oven for 20 minutes per 450 g (1 lb) plus 20 minutes extra, or less if you like your lamb very pink.

Remove from the oven, transfer the meat to a warm dish and keep warm. To make the gravy, strain off most of the fat in the roasting tin, reserving all the cooking juices. Fry the sliced onion in the fat and cooking juices, until soft and just turning brown. Sprinkle in the flour and cook for 1–2 minutes more, then remove from the heat and stir in the stock. Put back on the heat and add blackcurrant jelly to taste. Bring to the boil, stirring frequently, and continue boiling briskly for about 2 minutes. Taste and season as necessary, then sharpen with the red wine. Remove from the heat and strain.

Thickly slice the lamb and arrange on a warm serving dish. Spoon over a little of the gravy and garnish with fresh mint. Serve the rest of the gravy separately. (Serves 4–6)

Stuffed loin of lamb at the Lakeside Hotel, Newby Bridge, with a view of Windermere beyond

ROAST HERDWICK LAMB WITH ONION AND THYME SAUCE

In 1924 Beatrix Potter began to invest the income from her books in the breeding of pedigree Herdwick sheep, buying a large fell farm, Troutbeck Park. She invited shepherd Tom Storey to improve the farm and build up the flocks of this local hardy breed which she so loved. The Herdwick is prized not only for its meat, but for its wool, which is particularly hard-wearing.

Beatrix had become closely interested in the work of the National Trust and when she died, left fifteen farms to them in her will, specifying that the sheep on her fell farms should be pure Herdwicks. She would be delighted to know that the National Trust now produce fishermen's crewnecks, slipovers, slippers, ties and wallets – all made of Herdwick wool.

For this recipe any lamb may be used if you are unable to get hold of Herdwick.

2.5–2.7 kg (5–6 lb) leg of Herdwick lamb
2 large cloves of garlic, sliced
75 g (3 oz/6 US tablespoons) softened butter
Freshly milled sea salt and black pepper
Onion skins
1 large carrot, sliced
3–4 sprigs of fresh thyme
1 teaspoon wholemeal flour
300 ml (½ pint/1¼ cups) lamb stock (made from the knuckle end)
150 ml (¼ pint/⅔ cup) red wine

For the sauce

40 g (1½ oz/3 US tablespoons) butter
1 large onion, finely chopped (reserve the skins)
25 g (1 oz/3 US tablespoons) plain white flour
150 ml (¼ pint/⅔ cup) milk
150 ml (¼ pint/⅔ cup) stock or water
1 tablespoon chopped fresh thyme or 1 teaspoon dried
150 ml (¼ pint/⅔ cup) double cream or crème fraîche
Salt and freshly milled black pepper

Pre-heat the oven to 230°C (450°F, gas mark 8).

Cut the knuckle end off the leg of lamb to make stock. Then wipe the meat with the absorbent kitchen paper and spike with pieces of garlic. Coat liberally with the butter and season well with salt and pepper. Place the onion skins and carrot on the bottom of a roasting tin and put the leg on top. Add the thyme on top of the joint and roast in a hot oven for about 1½ hours, basting every 30 minutes. Transfer the meat to a warm serving dish and keep hot while you make the gravy.

The sauce can be made while the meat is cooking. Melt the butter in a pan and cook the onion for about 10 minutes until soft, but not coloured. Stir in the flour and cook for 1–2 minutes, then remove from the heat and gradually add the milk, stock or water, and the thyme. Cook gently again until smooth and thick, then simmer very slowly for about 5 minutes. Just before serving, stir in the cream and season to taste with salt and pepper.

To make the gravy, pour off any excess fat from the roasting tin, reserving the onion skins, carrot slices and cooking juices. Stir a little flour into the juices and vegetables and cook for a few minutes over moderate heat. Remove from the heat and gradually add the stock and wine. Stir well, then cook over moderate heat until thick and smooth. Season to taste, then strain into a gravy boat.

Serve the lamb carved in thick slices, with the gravy and sauce served separately. Accompany with roast or new potatoes, or Gloucester cheese stew (see page 82) and other vegetables. (Serves 6)

Variation

LEEK-AND-THYME SAUCE

Substitute 2 medium leeks instead of the onion and make as before.

STICKY BRAISED OXTAIL WITH PRUNES

When Beatrix Potter, or Mrs Heelis as she was widely known, became the owner of Troutbeck Park Farm, she began to improve the local stock of Herdwick sheep but she also reared Galloway cattle from stock bought at Newcastleton on the Borders, for beef of good quality. This recipe is just the type of meaty dish that Beatrix and her husband Willie Heelis loved. As their surviving Sawrey neighbours remember, they enjoyed old-fashioned meals like hot-pots, stews and meat pies, with a joint of roast beef on most Sundays. Oxtail is probably the most under-rated cut of meat, but nothing produces such rib-sticking winter braises; best for being made and then re-heated one or two days later. This allows time for the flavour to develop.

12 large pieces of oxtail
225 ml (7½ fl oz/scant 1 cup) red wine
225 ml (7½ fl oz/scant 1 cup) elderberry wine or port
1 large onion, sliced
3 large carrots, roughly chopped
12 large prunes
1 large sprig of fresh thyme or a pinch of dried
1 bay leaf
2 strips of orange peel
600 ml (1 pint/2½ cups) prune soaking liquor and beef stock
Salt and freshly milled black pepper
A little chopped fresh parsley, to garnish

Trim the pieces of oxtail of excess fat. Place in a large bowl with the wines, onion and carrots. Leave in a cool place for 6–8 hours, turning the meat occasionally. At the same time, place the prunes in another bowl, cover with cold water and leave to soak.

Pre-heat the oven to 140°C (275°F, gas mark 1).

Transfer the oxtail to a heavy casserole dish with all the marinade ingredients. Add the thyme, bay leaf and orange peel, then pour over the prune soaking liquor made up to the required amount with beef stock or water. Season with salt and pepper. Bring gently to the boil, then cover tightly with a sheet of greaseproof paper between dish and lid. Cook in a slow oven for 3–3½ hours. Turn off the oven and leave to cool in the oven. Refrigerate overnight.

Next day, pre-heat the oven to 200°C (400°F, gas mark 6). Remove all the surface fat. Heat until the jellied sauce melts, then transfer the meat, onion and carrots to a shallow ovenproof dish.

Strain the sauce into a clean pan and reduce over a moderately high heat by about a quarter, or until well-flavoured, skimming often. Adjust seasoning as necessary. Pour over the oxtail and surround with prunes. Cook in a fairly hot oven for about 40 minutes, basting occasionally and turning the meat half way through, until nicely glazed and brown. Thicken juices slightly if necessary.

Serve sprinkled with parsley, with mashed or boiled potatoes and crisp winter cabbage. (Serves 6)

STEAK, KIDNEY AND OYSTER PUDDING WITH A GUINNESS GRAVY

Here is another traditional country dish. This is a modern version, with just a light pastry crust on top rather than lining the whole pudding. The addition of oysters or mussels doesn't give a fishy taste, but enriches the gravy. Fresh field mushrooms give a better flavour, but obviously cultivated mushrooms can be used, preferably the large dark variety.

900 g (2 lb) rump steak (top round or top sirloin), trimmed of all fat and sinew
450 g (1 lb) veal or lamb kidney
25 g (1 oz/2 US tablespoons) butter
1 tablespoon sunflower oil
2 large onions, sliced
1 clove of garlic, halved

125 g (4 oz/1½ cups) sliced wild mushrooms or large cultivated mushrooms
2 sprigs of fresh thyme or ½ teaspoon dried
600 ml (1 pint/2½ cups) Guinness
Salt and freshly milled black pepper
12 fresh or canned oysters or mussels (optional)

For the pastry

150 g (5 oz/1 cup) self-raising flour
1 level teaspoon baking powder
1 level teaspoon salt
Freshly milled white pepper
Large pinch of ground mace
1 tablespoon finely grated lemon rind
1 tablespoon chopped fresh parsley
75 g (3 oz/6 US tablespoons) cold, hard butter
1 standard (medium) egg
2 (3 US) tablespoons ice-cold water

Start to pre-cook the meat the day before you wish to serve the pudding.

Pre-heat the oven to 170°C (325°F, gas mark 3).

Cut the meat and kidney into 2.5-cm (1-in) cubes. Heat the butter and oil together in a frying pan until smoking, then fry the meat and kidney in small batches, until evenly brown all over. Using a slotted spoon, transfer to an ovenproof casserole dish. Fry the onions in the remaining fat until brown, then put in the casserole dish. Add the garlic, mushrooms and thyme and pour over the Guinness. Season well with salt and pepper, then cover with a lid and cook in a slow oven for 1½–2 hours. Remove from the oven and leave to cool overnight.

Next day, transfer the meat to a 1–1.75-litre (2–3-pint/2-quart US) pudding basin, layering it with the oysters. Taste and adjust the seasoning as necessary.

To make the crust, sieve the flour with the baking powder, salt, pepper and mace. Mix in the lemon rind and parsley, then grate the butter on the coarse side of the grater. Gently rub it into the dry ingredients. Beat the egg with the water, then, using a fork, add it to the flour mixture to form a softish dough. Turn on to a lightly floured surface, knead very lightly, then pat out to make a circle which will just fit *inside* the top of the basin. Cover with buttered greaseproof paper, pleated across the top to allow room for expansion, then pleated foil. Tie both layers down securely with string and steam the pudding for about 2 hours.

When ready to serve, remove the paper and foil, wrap a clean napkin around the basin and place it on a serving dish. Cut a wedge of the crust top for each person and serve with a generous helping of the filling. (Serves 6)

HIGHLAND KIDNEYS

In traditional sheep-rearing areas, many recipes can be found for every single part of the sheep. This is just one, which has a Scottish flavour. Try and buy kidneys in their suet, because the flavour is so much better.

18 lambs' kidneys
Seasoned flour
75 g (3 oz/6 US tablespoons) butter
1 medium onion, finely chopped
3 smoked back bacon rashers (6 slices Canadian bacon) chopped
1½ (2 US) tablespoons chopped fresh rosemary or 1½ teaspoons dried
225 ml (7½ fl oz/scant 1 cup) single cream
4 tablespoons (⅓ cup) Drambuie or whisky
Salt and freshly milled black pepper
Tiny sprigs of fresh rosemary, to garnish
A few marigold petals, to garnish

Skin the kidneys, then cut each one in half lengthways. Snip out the cores with scissors, then dust in seasoned flour.

Heat the butter in a large frying pan and fry the onion and bacon for about 5 minutes. Add the kidneys and rosemary and fry gently for 5 minutes, until the kidneys are sealed and brown on all sides, stirring occasionally.

Stir in the cream and liqueur and season to taste with salt and pepper. Bring to the boil, then simmer gently until the sauce has thickened and the kidneys are tender. Garnish with a few sprigs of rosemary and sprinkle with marigold petals.

Serve hot with rice, mashed potatoes or noodles and a mixed salad. (Serves 6)

SCOTTISH BRIDIES

Bridies are Scottish pasties containing beef (said to be the best beef of all Britain, since this is Aberdeen-Angus country) or lamb. The recipe took its name, apparently, from a particularly successful maker of the pasties: Margaret Bridie of Glamis.
Beatrix Potter wrote in her journal of going out to lunch with her father in Perth while they were on holiday: 'Had a large lunch for ten-pence, "Cookies", "Bridies" and lemonade at Woods.' She also observed the local Aberdeen-Angus cattle during her Scottish summer holidays. In September 1892 she writes in her journal about the practice of dehorning, which had become more popular; Beatrix disapproved of the effect this had on the animal's appearance: 'the result is an idiotic beast with great flapping ears'.

For the pastry

700 g (1½ lb/5 cups) plain white or wholemeal flour
Large pinch of salt
175 g (6 oz/¾ cup) lard
175 g (6 oz/¾ cup) butter or margarine
Ice-cold water, to mix
Beaten egg and milk, to glaze

For the filling

700 g (1½ lb) rump steak (top round steak or top sirloin)
125 g (4 oz) suet, finely chopped
175 g (6 oz) onion, finely chopped
Salt and freshly milled black pepper
A little prepared mustard

To make the pastry, sieve the flour and salt together into a large mixing bowl. Cut the fats into the flour, then rub in with your fingertips until the mixture looks like breadcrumbs. Gradually add enough iced water to make a stiff dough, then knead lightly until it is smooth. Place in a polythene bag and leave to rest in the fridge for at least 30 minutes.

Pre-heat the oven to 200°C (400°F, gas mark 6).

Beat the meat with a mallet or rolling pin and cut into 12-mm (½-in) strips. Mix with the suet and onion, then season well with salt, pepper and a little mustard.

Divide the prepared pastry into 6 pieces and roll out on a lightly floured surface into 6 oval shapes. Divide the meat mixture evenly between each oval and place on one half. Fold over the free half of pastry, press the edges together firmly and pinch them with a slight twist to form a good seal. Make two small holes in the top of each bridie to let the steam escape during cooking. Brush with beaten egg and milk and place on a greased baking tray.

Bake in a fairly hot oven for 10 minutes, then reduce the temperature to 180°C (350°F, gas mark 4) and cook for a further 30–35 minutes, until the meat is cooked and the pastry is golden brown.

Bridies are delicious served hot or cold, and if wrapped in a clean cloth or foil straight from the oven will keep warm for some time. They are excellent for a picnic lunch, and they make a popular snack for taking fell-walking, hunting or hound-trailing (Serves 6).

Scottish farm land photographed by Beatrix's father, Rupert Potter, in September 1893

53

CUMBERLAND SAUSAGE WITH APPLE, SAGE AND ONION SAUCE

Cumberland sausage is a fine traditional delicacy. It is made solely from fresh pork, herbs and seasoning, with each butcher having his own recipe. Unlike the usual sausage, the Cumberland variety is not twisted into links but made in one continuous coil, sometimes up to four feet long, from which the required amount is cut off. Because the two ends are open, it is best to bake it.

Cumberland sausage is one of the popular dishes served at the Tower Bank Arms in Near Sawrey, the pub that features in The Tale of Jemima Puddle-Duck. *Willow Taylor, daughter of Margaret and William Burns, who ran the pub for thirty-five years, tells me that her mother was very friendly with Beatrix Potter and chatted most days over the fence at Hill Top. Apparently she only came into the Tower Bank Arms 'when she wanted to tell my father that I'd been a naughty girl!' Beatrix was, in her own words, 'a total abstainer'. One night there was a sing-song in the pub with Lakeland hunting songs from the village folk to celebrate a John Peel anniversary; Beatrix would not go into the building, but paced up and down outside, listening to the music.*

900 g–1 kg (2–2¼ lb) Cumberland sausage
1 small cooking apple
50 g (2 oz/¼ cup) lard or dripping

For the sauce

25 g (1 oz/2 US tablespoons) butter
½ medium onion, finely chopped
450 g (1 lb) Cox's apples or other firm eating apples
Small clove of garlic, crushed
1 tablespoon chopped fresh sage or 1 teaspoon dried
1 tablespoon water
Juice of ½ lemon
Salt and freshly milled black pepper

Pre-heat the oven to 180°C (350°F, gas mark 4).

Place the coil of sausage in a greased baking tin and put the apple in the centre of the coil. Prick the sausage with a fork every 7.5 cm (3 in) and dot with fat. Bake in the centre of a moderate oven for about 1 hour, or until the juices run clear, turning the sausage once or twice during the cooking time.

To make the sauce, heat the butter in a pan and fry the onion until golden brown. Peel, core and chop the apples and add to the pan with the garlic and sage. Fry gently for 1–2 minutes, then add the water and lemon juice. Simmer for 15–20 minutes, or until soft and fluffy, then remove from the heat and beat well. (Reduce to a purée in a blender or processor if you wish.) Season with salt and pepper.

Serve the sausage with some cooked potatoes fried in the pan juices or mashed potatoes, and hot beetroot or red cabbage. Accompany with the warm sauce and Cumberland mustard. (Serves 6)

Right: Cumberland sausage at the Tower Bank Arms
Below: Willow Taylor. The Tower Bank Arms, where she lived as a little girl, can be seen in the background

DUCHESS'S VEAL AND HAM PIE

Sawrey animals and Sawrey village are remembered in Beatrix Potter's story The Tale of The Pie and The Patty-Pan. *Ribby was a Sawrey cat and Duchess was an amalgamation of two pedigree Pomeranians belonging to Mrs Rogerson, later to be Beatrix's housekeeper at Castle Cottage. The book took much longer to finish than Beatrix had planned. 'I don't think I have ever seriously considered the state of the pie, but I think the book runs some risk of being over-cooked if it goes on much longer!' she wrote to her editor, Norman Warne.*

Perhaps the veal and ham pie which Duchess took to Ribby's tea party was similar to this one. I am sure she would enjoy the lovely firm, meaty filling, and surprise centre of hard-boiled egg – no patty-pan in sight!

For the stock

450 g (1 lb) veal and pork bones
1 medium onion, roughly chopped
1 medium carrot, roughly chopped
1 stick of celery, chopped
1 bay leaf
Salt and freshly milled black pepper
Cold water, to cover

For the filling

450 g (1 lb) veal fillet or pie-veal (veal stew meat)
1 tablespoon chopped fresh parsley
1 tablespoon chopped fresh mint
Pinch of dried marjoram
½ teaspoon ground mace
Finely grated rind of 1 lemon
2 medium onions, finely chopped
1 teaspoon salt
Large pinch freshly milled black pepper
125 g (4 oz) cooked ham or gammon, in thick slices
3 large eggs, hard-boiled
300 ml (½ pint/1¼ cups) jellied stock (see above)

For the pastry

350 g (12 oz/2½ cups) plain wholemeal flour
½ teaspoon salt
Large pinch of ground mace
1 egg yolk
125 g (4 oz/½ cup) lard
120 ml (4 fl oz/½ cup) water
90 ml (3 fl oz/⅓ cup) milk
Beaten egg, to glaze

To make the stock, put the veal and pork bones into a large pan with the vegetables. Cover with water, then add the bay leaf. Season lightly, then bring to the boil. Cover and simmer for 1½ hours. Strain and return to the pan, then boil rapidly until reduced to 300 ml (½ pint/1¼ cups). Allow the stock to cool, then chill until set and jellied.

Grease a 1.5-litre (2½-pint/8 in × 4 in) loaf tin and line the base with greased greaseproof paper. If using pie-veal, trim it very carefully and remove all the skin and fat. Mince the veal and mix with the parsley, mint, marjoram, mace, lemon rind, onion and salt and pepper in a large bowl. Cut the ham into strips.

To make the pastry, sieve the flour, salt and mace into a warm mixing bowl. Make a well in the centre and add the egg yolk. Put the lard, water and milk in a saucepan and gently heat until the lard has melted. Bring to the boil, then pour immediately into the well in the flour and draw the ingredients together with a wooden spoon to form a soft, pliable (but not sticky) dough.

Transfer to a lightly floured surface and knead until smooth and elastic. Put the dough back in the bowl and cover with a damp cloth. Rest in a warm place for 20 minutes, until the dough is easy to work, but do not allow to cool completely before lining the tin.

Pre-heat the oven to 180°C (350°F, gas mark 4).

Pat two-thirds of the pastry evenly into the base and sides of the loaf tin. Press in half the veal mixture and cover with half the ham strips. Place the shelled hard-boiled eggs down the centre. Fill with the remaining veal mixture, then the rest of the ham.

Roll out the remaining dough to make a lid for the pie. Brush the edges of the pastry with water, then press on the lid; seal the edges well and crimp. Roll out the pastry trimmings to make leaves and so forth to decorate the lid, then make a large hole in the centre of the pie. Brush with beaten egg and bake in a moderate oven until the pastry has browned. Then reduce the temperature to 160°C (325°F, gas mark 3) and continue to cook for a total time in the oven of 1¾–2 hours. Cover the pastry with foil towards the end of the cooking time if it is over-browning.

Remove from the oven and leave to cool in the tin for about 4 hours. Then, place the jellied stock in a pan and bring almost to the boil. Taste and adjust the seasoning as necessary, then allow to cool for about 10 minutes. Pour through the hole in the pastry lid of the pie, using a small funnel. Leave the pie in a cool place for about 1 hour (not the fridge), then leave at room temperature for a further 1 hour.

Remove from the tin and serve cut in thick slices with salad – traditionally at a picnic. (Serves 6)

*C*HEESE-CRUSTED HAM AND LEEK ROLLS

Norman Warne, Beatrix Potter's editor, suggested that Beatrix might like to copy the dolls' house he had made for his niece, Winifred, for her Tale of Two Bad Mice. *He sent Beatrix 'the little stove & the ham', toy food from Hamley's shop, for inspiration.*

300 ml (½ pint/1¼ cups) chicken stock
6 young leeks, washed and trimmed
6 thin slices good quality ham
A little Cumberland or mild wholegrain mustard
50 g (2 oz/¼ cup) butter
1½ (2 US) tablespoons plain flour
200 ml (7 fl oz/⅞ cup) double cream or crème fraîche
125 g (4 oz/½ cup) grated farmhouse Cheddar cheese
Salt and freshly milled black pepper
Freshly grated nutmeg
2–3 tablespoons (¼ cup) fresh wholemeal
breadcrumbs

Put the chicken stock in a pan large enough to hold the leeks and bring to the boil. Arrange the leeks in the pan, bring back to the boil, then simmer for 8–10 minutes, or until the leeks are just tender. Drain them thoroughly, reserving the cooking liquor.

Pre-heat the oven to 200°C (400°F, gas mark 6).

Spread each slice of ham with a little mustard and wrap around a leek. Arrange the rolls, flap-side down, in a buttered ovenproof dish.

Melt 40 g (1½ oz/3 tablespoons) of the butter in a pan and stir in the flour. Cook for 1–2 minutes, then remove from the heat. Gradually add 240 ml (8 fl oz/ 1 cup) of the leek cooking liquor, then cook gently, stirring continuously, until thick and smooth. Bring to the boil, then stir in the cream. Bring back to the boil and then remove from the heat. Beat in 45 ml (3 tablespoons/¼ cup) of the cheese and season to taste with salt, pepper and plenty of nutmeg. Pour this sauce over the leek and ham rolls. Mix the remaining cheese with the breadcrumbs and sprinkle over the top of the sauce. Dot with small pieces of the remaining butter.

Bake in a fairly hot oven for 20–30 minutes, or until hot and bubbling with a golden brown top. Serve with crusty wholemeal bread or soda bread for lunch or supper. (Serves 6)

Variation

*C*HEESE-CRUSTED HAM AND CHICORY ROLLS

Substitute 6 fat heads of chicory for the leeks.

From The Tale of Two Bad Mice

*C*UMBERLAND PORK LOAF

The first British 'country house hotel' was Sharrow Bay, a rambling Cumbrian lodge on the remote north-eastern tip of Ullswater. Today it is run by Francis Coulson and Brian Sack. Mr Coulson has refined a repertoire of traditional Lakeland dishes and the hotel has become one of the most famous and popular in the area.
This recipe, using traditional Cumbrian delicacies, is served regularly at the Sharrow Bay.

50 g (2 oz/½ cup) stale white breadcrumbs
150 ml (¼ pint/⅔ cup) milk
700 g (1½ lb) lean pork, minced
250 g (8 oz) Cumberland sausagemeat
1 large egg, beaten
Salt and freshly milled black pepper
1 tablespoon chopped fresh parsley
4 bay leaves

For the sauce

4 tablespoons (⅓ cup) redcurrant jelly
4 tablespoons (⅓ cup) demerara sugar
Finely grated rind of 1 orange
2 (3 US) tablespoons orange juice
2 teaspoons prepared Cumberland or
wholegrain mustard

Soak the breadcrumbs in the milk until soft and pulpy. Mix the minced pork, sausagemeat, soaked breadcrumbs and beaten egg in a large bowl. Season with salt and pepper and add the parsley, mixing well again.

To make the sauce, blend all the ingredients together in a bowl. Spread the sauce over the bottom of a greased 900-g (2-lb/9 in × 5 in) loaf tin, then spoon in the meat mixture. Pack down firmly, then arrange the bay leaves on top.

Pre-heat the oven to 180°C (350°F, gas mark 4).

Cover the tin with kitchen foil and bake in a moderate oven for 1 hour, or until cooked. Remove and discard the bay leaves, then pour off the juices into a warm sauceboat. Turn out the pork loaf on to a warm serving dish and serve immediately with the sauce.

The loaf is also excellent served cold, with cold sauce, for a summer lunch or picnic. (Serves 6)

Left: Cumberland pork loaf at the Sharrow Bay Hotel on Ullswater

Above: Beatrix Potter's farm pigs sketched as background studies for The Tale of Pigling Bland

PORK CHOPS IN CIDER WITH FRESH SAGE

---

*Beatrix Potter was very fond of pigs, pink or black.
She wrote from Hill Top in 1907 to Louie Warne, one of the
Warne publishing family, 'I have got two lovely pigs, one is
a little bigger than the other, she is very fat and black with
a very turned up nose and the fattest cheeks I ever saw; she
likes being tickled under the chin, she is a very friendly pig.
I call her Aunt Susan. I call the smaller pig Dorcas; she is
not so tame, she runs round & round the pig stye.'*

*By August the following year Beatrix had
fourteen pigs. Of course, as a farmer she couldn't be too
sentimental, and sent baby pork to her publishers at
Christmas. She wrote, 'The poor little cherub had such a
sweet smile . . . It is rather a shame to kill them so young.'
Beatrix's feelings overcame her better judgement, however,
in the matter of Pig-wig, 'a perfectly lovely little black
Berkshire pig', whom she first met at Hard Cragg when
fetching pigs for John Cannon from Farmer Townley.
Cannon refused to take the 'tiny black girl-pig', so Pig-wig
became a household pet, bottle-fed and kept in a basket by
the bed.*

*During a long illness before her marriage to Willie Heelis,
Beatrix worked on* The Tale of Pigling Bland, *using the
pigs at Hill Top and Castle Cottage Farm as models.*

6 pork or bacon chops
Salt and freshly milled black pepper
12 finely chopped fresh sage leaves
or 1 teaspoon dried
2 large onions, sliced
2 large cloves of garlic, crushed
A little butter if necessary
3 crisp tart eating apples, peeled, cored and sliced
225 ml (7½ fl oz/scant 1 cup) still dry cider
3 tablespoons (¼ cup) apple brandy or
brandy (optional)
150 ml (¼ pint/⅔ cup) double cream or crème fraîche
150 ml (¼ pint/⅔ cup) sour cream or natural yoghurt

For the garnish

75 g (3 oz/6 US tablespoons) butter
3 crisp eating apples, unpeeled and thickly sliced
40 g (1½ oz/3 US tablespoons) sugar
1 small bunch watercress
50 g (2 oz/⅓ cup) chopped walnuts (optional)

Pre-heat the oven to 180°C (350°F, gas mark 4).

Remove the skin and surplus fat from the chops, reserving the fat. Season well with salt and pepper on both sides. Dice the fat finely and melt it in a frying pan. Quickly brown the chops on both sides and, using a slotted spoon, transfer them to a shallow casserole dish. Sprinkle with the sage.

Fry the onions and garlic for about 5 minutes until soft, adding a little butter if necessary, then add to the meat in the casserole dish. Fry the apples for a few seconds on each side, then place a few slices over each chop. Pour the cider into the frying pan and bring to the boil. Simmer for a few minutes to incorporate cooking juices, then pour over the chops. Cover the casserole tightly and cook in a moderate oven for about 40 minutes, or until the chops are tender.

Strain the cooking liquor through a sieve into a pan, keeping the chops warm on a serving dish. Add the brandy to the cooking liquor and bring to the boil. Continue boiling rapidly for a few minutes to reduce a little, then add the creams. Stir well, then bring back to the boil for 1 minute. Taste and adjust the seasoning as necessary and keep warm.

To prepare the garnish, heat the butter in a frying pan. Dip one side of each apple slice in the sugar. Cook the apple slices, sugared side down, in the hot butter over high heat for 4–5 minutes, or until the sugar caramelises. Sprinkle the rest of the sugar on the apples, turn over and cook for 4–5 minutes.

Spoon the sauce over the pork and garnish the dish with the caramelised apple slices and watercress. Sprinkle with walnuts. Serve with crusty wholemeal bread, new potatoes, rice or noodles, and a green vegetable or green salad. (Serves 6)

*S*UGAR-BAKED CUMBERLAND HAM

Beatrix's husband, Willie Heelis, was very particular about his breakfast bacon, insisting that the rasher be started in a smoking hot frying-pan and not a cold one. He and Beatrix cured their own hams in the cellar at Castle Cottage, salting the pigs' legs on a slate slab. Favoured friends, if piglets were numerous, were presented with a sucking pig at Christmas.

Beatrix wrote to Millie Warne just before Christmas in 1916 telling her that the lady in the village shop had sold poor Willie cream of tartar instead of saltpetre for curing the hams. 'He rubbed it on the hams. It discoloured them, but I hope it may not have done any harm, as the mistake was found out and the hams washed.'

This recipe for cooking ham is recommended by Richard Woodall of Waberthwaite, whose family has been famous for its home-cured Cumberland hams for seven generations. He also claims to be the first British producer of Parma-style air-dried ham, which has herbs added during the curing process before it is air dried for at least 12 months.

From The Tale of Little Pig Robinson

1 uncooked ham (5–7.6 kg/11–17 lb)
175–225 g (6–8 oz) demerara sugar

Soak the ham in cold water for at least 24 hours, then scrape or scrub off the rust or bloom before cooking.

Pre-heat the oven to 190°C (375°F, gas mark 5).

Drain off the water, rinse well and dry the ham with a clean tea-towel. Wrap it in a flour and water dough or kitchen foil. Place in a large roasting tin and bake it in the oven, allowing 15 minutes to the 450 g (1 lb).

Remove from the oven and leave the ham in its crust or foil until luke-warm. Unwrap the foil or break open the crust with a rolling pin. Strip off the skin and sprinkle generously with sugar.

Place under a hot grill until golden brown, then serve hot or cold decorated as you wish. (Serves approximately 24)

Poultry and Game

Country Pot-Roasted Chicken 64

Castle Cottage Turkey 64

Derwentwater Wild Duckling with Cumberland Sauce 65

Roast Duck with Apricot Sauce 66

Roast Goose with Sage, Onion and Damson Stuffing 68

Roast Grouse with Whisky and Marmalade Sauce 69

Pheasant with Port, Orange and Chestnuts 69

Roast Pheasant with Rowan Jelly 70

Ees Wyke Partridge 72

Pigeons in a Pot with Red Cabbage and Damsons 72

Beefsteak, Pigeon and Mushroom Pudding 73

Casserole of Venison with Juniper Berries 75

Huntsman's Pot 75

Rabbit Casserole with Cheese and Herb Dumplings 76

Old English Rabbit Pie 77

COUNTRY POT-ROASTED CHICKEN

When Beatrix Potter bought Hill Top in the Lake District village of Near Sawrey in 1905 she also bought 'some nice little chickens'. Mrs Cannon, the farm manager's wife, is to be seen feeding the poultry in a picture in The Tale of Jemima Puddle-Duck.

1.5–1.8 kg (3½–4 lb) free-range chicken, with giblets
2-3 (3–4 US) tablespoons olive oil
1 medium onion, roughly chopped
6 button onions
1 head of garlic, cleaned but not peeled
2 carrots, sliced
1 bulb of fennel, roughly chopped
1 bay leaf
700 g (1½ lb) small new potatoes, scraped
150 ml (¼ pint/⅔ cup) dry white wine
300 ml (½ pint/1¼ cups) chicken stock (made with the giblets)
Salt and freshly milled black pepper
40 g (1½ oz/3 US tablespoons) butter
40 g (1½ oz/⅓ cup) plain flour

Pre-heat the oven to 180°C (350°F, gas mark 4).

Wipe the cavity of the chicken with absorbent kitchen paper. Heat a little of the oil in a large, flameproof casserole dish and fry the chopped onion, button onions and garlic until soft and coloured a little. Remove with a slotted spoon and reserve on one side.

Add more oil to the casserole dish and, when fairly hot, fry the chicken until evenly brown all over. Remove it from the casserole dish and keep on one side, then fry the carrots, fennel and bay leaf in the oil for about 5 minutes, or until slightly brown.

Meanwhile, par-boil the potatoes for 3–4 minutes. Drain and add them to the carrots and fennel in the casserole, with the reserved onions and garlic. Place the chicken on top, breast-side down, and pour in the wine and stock. Season well, then bring to simmering point. Cover very tightly and cook in a moderate oven for about 1½ hours, or until tender, turning the chicken over half-way through the time.

When the chicken is cooked, take the casserole from the oven. Remove the chicken carefully, tipping out the juices from the cavity into the rest of the sauce, and place it on a warmed serving dish. Surround the chicken with the well-drained vegetables, discarding the garlic and the bay leaf. Keep warm in the oven. Transfer the casserole dish to the top of the stove and boil for a few minutes to concentrate the flavour of the sauce. Remove from the heat. Make *beurre manié* by beating the butter and flour together, and add it in small pieces to the sauce. Bring back to the boil, whisking continuously until the sauce thickens. Taste and adjust the seasoning as necessary, then serve the chicken and vegetables with the sauce poured over them. (Serves 6)

CASTLE COTTAGE TURKEY

After her marriage Beatrix Potter kept ducks and turkeys, which she looked after herself. In a letter to Millie Warne, of the Warne publishing family, in December, 1916, Beatrix wrote, 'I shall be glad to get the turkeys safely off, and the horrid slaughter over, poor dears they are so tame and tractable, but they do eat.'

3 turkey breast fillets each weighing about 250 g (8 oz), skinned and halved
Seasoned flour
25 g (1 oz/2 US tablespoons) butter
1½ tablespoons sunflower oil
1 small onion, finely sliced
1 large clove of garlic, crushed
175 g (6 oz) chanterelle or oyster mushrooms, sliced
450 ml (¾ pint/scant 2 cups) chicken stock
Finely grated rind and juice of 1 lime
1½ teaspoons chopped fresh tarragon or ¾ teaspoon dried
4 (5 US) tablespoons dry white wine
200 ml (7 fl oz/⅞ cup) double cream or crème fraîche
Salt and freshly milled black pepper
Sprigs of fresh tarragon, to garnish

Coat each halved turkey breast in seasoned flour. Heat the butter and oil in a large frying pan and fry the turkey until lightly browned on both sides. Remove with a slotted spoon and put on one side. Soften the onion in the remaining fat, then add the garlic and mushrooms, chicken stock, rind and juice of the lime, tarragon and wine. Replace the turkey in the pan, cover and cook gently for about 20 minutes, or until tender. Stir in the cream and season to taste.

Serve garnished with fresh tarragon and accompany with new potatoes and a green vegetable. (Serves 6)

DERWENTWATER WILD DUCKLING WITH CUMBERLAND SAUCE

The wild duck of Derwentwater in Lakeland are famous for their tenderness and flavour. Beatrix loved the lake and surrounding areas and sketched many local views, which she later used in her books.
The recipe is based on one from The Mill Hotel, Mungrisdale.

3 wild ducks, weighing 900 g–1.4 kg (2–3 lb) each
25 g (1 oz/2 US tablespoons) butter, melted
9 green streaky bacon rashers
Juice of 1 large lemon
Salt and freshly milled black pepper
Lemon and orange slices, to garnish
Watercress, to garnish

For the sauce

Grated rind and juice of 1 large orange
Finely grated rind and juice of 1 large lemon
350 g (12 oz/1½ cups) redcurrant jelly
150 ml (¼ pint/⅔ cup) port
1 teaspoon English mustard powder
1 teaspoon ground ginger
A little arrowroot blended with cold water, to thicken

Pre-heat the oven to 200°C (400°F, gas mark 6).

Wipe the ducks inside and out with absorbent kitchen paper, then place in a roasting tin. Brush them all over with the melted butter, then cover the breasts with streaky bacon. Roast in a fairly hot oven for about 45 minutes, basting once or twice during this time. Remove the bacon and continue to cook until the birds are done to your liking (7–15 minutes).

Transfer the ducks to a warmed serving dish, score along the breastbone 2 or 3 times and sprinkle over the lemon juice. Season with a little salt and pepper, cover with foil and keep warm until ready to serve.

While the ducks are cooking, make the sauce. Put the finely shredded orange and lemon rind in a small saucepan with enough water to cover. Bring to the boil, cover and simmer gently for 4–5 minutes. Drain through a sieve and refresh with cold water. Drain again and set aside. Put the redcurrant jelly and port into a saucepan and bring slowly to the boil, stirring occasionally so that the jelly dissolves. Mix the mustard powder and ginger together in a basin. Add a little of the lemon juice and mix to form a paste. Slowly add the rest of the lemon juice, followed by the orange juice, stirring all the time. Add the redcurrant and port mixture through a sieve and finally stir in the shreds of orange and lemon rind. Stir well and return to the saucepan. Reheat gently, thickening with some arrowroot blended with a little cold water.

Serve the ducks garnished with watercress and lemon and orange slices, handing round the Cumberland sauce separately (half a bird to each person). An endive and orange salad is an ideal accompaniment for this dish (see page 102). (Serves 6)

Variations

Domesticated duckling or duckling portions may be used instead of wild. Cook whole duckling for 30 minutes per 450 g/1 lb at 180°C (350°F, gas mark 4) and portions for 1–1¼ hours.

ROAST DUCK WITH APRICOT SAUCE

*You need a large duck to feed 6 people (allow 450 g [1 lb]
for each person); if this is not possible, cook 2 smaller ducks
or joints. The apricot sauce recipe comes from Jean
Butterworth of Grasmere, who, with her husband, used to
to run the White Moss House Hotel at Rydal Water.*

1 large oven-ready duck, weighing about 3 kg
(6½–7 lb), with giblets
Salt and freshly milled black pepper
Sprigs of fresh tarragon or other fresh herbs,
to garnish
Apricot halves, to garnish

For the stuffing (optional)

50 g (2 oz/¼ cup) butter
250 g (8 oz) onion, finely chopped
125 g (4 oz/⅔ cup) finely chopped mushrooms
1 duck liver
125 g (4 oz/1⅓ cups) fresh wholemeal breadcrumbs
Finely grated rind of 1 lemon
2 (3 US) tablespoons fresh tarragon
or 2 teaspoons dried
1 egg, beaten
1–2 tablespoons stock
Salt and freshly milled black pepper

For the sauce

450 g (1 lb) cooked fresh or dried apricots or tinned
apricots (in natural juice), drained
1 teaspoon ground ginger
1 teaspoon ground cinnamon
150 ml (¼ pint/⅔ cup) Madeira or sherry
Salt and freshly milled black pepper

To make the stuffing, if using, melt the butter in a
frying pan and cook the onion gently for about 5
minutes, then add the mushrooms. Continue to fry
for a further 5 minutes until soft and just browned.
Remove with a slotted spoon to a mixing bowl and
fry the duck liver quickly in the same pan. Chop
finely and add to the onion mixture with the breadcrumbs, lemon rind and tarragon. Bind together with
the egg and stock and season to taste.

Pre-heat the oven to 180°C (350°F, gas mark 4).

Wipe the duck inside and out with absorbent
kitchen paper and pat the skin dry so that it will crisp
well during cooking. Spoon the stuffing into the
body cavity and secure with small skewers. Weigh to
calculate the cooking time, then place the duck,
breast-side up, on a rack in a roasting tin and prick
the skin all over with a cocktail stick or fork. Rub well
with salt and pepper to help crisp the skin. Roast for
30 minutes per 450 g (1 lb), increasing the oven
temperature to 200°C (400°F, gas mark 6) for the last
20 minutes to give a crisp brown finish to the skin.

For the sauce, purée the apricots in a blender or
food processor with the spices. Pour into a saucepan
and heat gently with the Madeira or sherry. Season to
taste with salt and pepper.

Transfer the duck to a warmed serving platter and
decorate with herbs and apricot halves. (Serves 6)

Right: Roast duck with apricot sauce
*Below: Peter and Sue Dixon, present owners of White Moss House, serve
their roast duck with damson sauce*

ROAST GOOSE WITH SAGE, ONION AND DAMSON STUFFING

The Postlethwaites of High Green Gate were near neighbours of Beatrix and Willie Heelis, of Castle Cottage. So close were the two houses that there could sometimes be territorial disputes! The geese belonging to the Postlethwaites once found their way into Beatrix's garden and began to crop the lawn. She told 'Possie', her nickname for Farmer Postlethwaite, to get his geese off her land before they ate all her grass. About two weeks later, the Heelis turkeys were grazing on Postlethwaite land. Mrs P. saw red, and so it went on.

Beatrix didn't keep geese herself, but I am sure she and Willie must have enjoyed the occasional Postlethwaite goose, roasted with sage and onion stuffing. Many traditional Lakeland cooks pop a few damsons or elderberries into stuffings, casseroles and savoury puddings. The addition of damsons to this stuffing works well, especially with the rich meat and skin of goose or duck. Plums or greengages could be used instead.

4–5 kg (9–11 lb) oven-ready goose, with giblets
Salt and freshly milled black pepper
Watercress, to garnish

For the stuffing

50 g (2 oz/¼ cup) butter
2 medium onions, finely chopped
1 clove of garlic, crushed
1 goose liver
175 g (6 oz/2 cups) fresh wholemeal breadcrumbs
3 teaspoons dried sage
250 g (8 oz) damsons, stoned and chopped
1 egg, beaten
A little stock
Salt and freshly milled black pepper

To make the stuffing, melt the butter in a frying pan and cook the onion and garlic gently for about 10 minutes, or until soft and lightly browned. Transfer to a mixing bowl. Fry the goose liver quickly until well browned, then chop finely and add to the onion mixture. Stir in the breadcrumbs, sage and chopped damsons, then bind together with egg and a little stock. Season well to taste.

Pre-heat the oven to 220°C (425°F, gas mark 7).

Wipe the bird inside and out with absorbent kitchen paper; pat the skin thoroughly dry so that it will crisp well during cooking. Spoon the stuffing into the body cavity. Secure with small skewers or sew up. Weigh the bird to calculate the cooking time.

Place the goose, breast-side up, on a rack in a roasting tin. Prick the skin all over with a cocktail stick or fork (don't stab too deeply into the flesh as this causes precious meat juices as well as fat to run out). Rub well with salt and black pepper. Roast near the top of a fairly hot oven for 30 minutes. Pour off the fat from the tin into a basin, turn the goose over, then reduce the oven temperature to 180°C (350°F, gas mark 4). Continue roasting for 1½ hours, then pour off the excess fat again and turn the goose over again (breast-side up). Continue roasting, allowing 15 minutes per 450 g (1 lb). Increase the oven temperature to 220°C (425°F, gas mark 7) for the last 20 minutes of the cooking time to give the skin a final crisping.

Test to see if the bird is cooked by piercing the thickest part of the thigh; if the juices run clear rather than pink, it is cooked. Remove the goose to a warmed serving platter and keep in a warm place for 10–15 minutes while making the gravy, using the cooking juices and stock made from the giblets. Serve garnished with plenty of watercress. (Serves 6)

Special note

Reserve all the excess fat from roasting the goose because it is excellent for frying and for making pastry. Farmers used to coat their boots with goose fat to protect them from wet and snowy weather and of course everyone knows about spreading one's chest with goose fat to ward off colds and flu!

Beatrix wrote from Hill Top in February, 1912: 'Conditions are Alpine — 24 degrees of frost last night . . . a pot of goose grease is in great request!!'

ROAST GROUSE WITH WHISKY AND MARMALADE SAUCE

Grouse shooting was one of the country pursuits followed by Beatrix's father, brother Bertram and visiting friends while the family were staying on holiday in Perthshire. Beatrix hated all field sports, so took herself off to sketch and photograph wild flowers and animals. Like her father, she had discovered the pleasure of photography. This recipe has a true Scottish flavour.

6 oven-ready grouse
1 large clove of garlic, halved
6 sprigs of fresh thyme or rosemary
6 small pieces of fresh bay leaf
3 tablespoons (¼ cup) sunflower oil
90 g (3½ oz/½ cup) butter
Salt and freshly milled black pepper
1 tablespoon soft brown sugar
24 baby onions, peeled
150 ml (¼ pint/⅔ cup) vegetable stock
350 g (12 oz) oyster, chestnut or field mushrooms
50 g (2 oz/¼ cup) butter, for frying
1 large clove of garlic, crushed
Small sprigs of fresh thyme or rosemary, to garnish

For the sauce

8 tablespoons (⅔ cup) Seville orange marmalade
(see page 155)
6 tablespoons (½ cup) malt whisky
Juice of 1 lemon

Pre-heat the oven to 200°C (400°F, gas mark 6).

Clean the cavity of each bird with absorbent kitchen paper, then rub the breasts with garlic and place a sprig of thyme and a piece of bay leaf inside each bird. Heat the oil and 40 g (1½ oz/3 table-spoons) of the butter in a large frying pan. Add the grouse and brown all over. Transfer with a slotted spoon to a roasting dish, season well and roast for 35–40 minutes, or until the breast meat is tender.

Meanwhile, heat the remaining butter with the sugar in the pan. Add the onions and stir over moderate heat until glazed and brown. Pour in the stock and continue to cook gently for about 15 minutes, or until the onions are soft and the stock has been absorbed. Keep warm.

Wipe the mushrooms, but do not wash them. Slice thickly. Melt the butter for frying in another pan, add the crushed garlic and stir in the mushrooms. Cook until golden, season and keep warm.

To make the sauce, melt the marmalade, then sieve it to remove the peel. Stir in the whisky and lemon juice. Keep warm.

Remove the grouse from the oven and cut each bird in half. Place two halves on 6 warmed serving plates. Divide the onions and mushrooms between the plates and spoon over a little sauce. Garnish with fresh thyme or rosemary. (Serves 6)

PHEASANT WITH PORT, ORANGE AND CHESTNUTS

Pheasant must have been on the menu many times while the Potter family was staying in Scotland or the Lake District for the summer holidays. This pheasant casserole is delicious served at a winter dinner party; excellent for Christmas.

2 large oven-ready pheasants
50 g (2 oz/¼ cup) butter
450 g (1 lb) chestnuts, shelled
250 g (8 oz) button onions
25 g (1 oz/3 US tablespoons) plain flour
600 ml (1 pint/2½ cups) game or chicken stock
Grated rind and juice of 1 orange
2 teaspoons redcurrant jelly
4 (5 US) tablespoons port
1 bouquet garni
Salt and freshly milled black pepper
40 g (1½ oz/3 US tablespoons) butter
40 g (1½ oz/⅓ cup) plain flour
Chopped fresh parsley
Fresh bay leaves, to garnish
Orange slices, to garnish

Roast pheasant with rowan jelly and (left) yarby pudden (see page 101 for recipe)

Pre-heat the oven to 180°C (350°F, gas mark 4).

Wipe the cavities of the pheasants with absorbent kitchen paper, then melt the butter in a large flame-proof casserole dish. Brown the pheasants all over in the butter, then remove using a slotted spoon and put on one side. Fry the chestnuts and onions gently in the casserole dish until just brown. Stir in the flour and cook for 1–2 minutes. Remove from the heat and gradually stir in the stock, orange rind and juice, redcurrant jelly and port. Add the bouquet garni and season to taste.

Return the pheasants to the casserole, cover and cook in a moderate oven for 1–1½ hours, or until the birds are tender.

To serve, divide the pheasants into joints, arrange on a warmed serving dish and keep warm. Make *beurre manié* by beating the butter and flour together. Transfer the casserole to the top of the stove, discard the bouquet garni and thicken the sauce by adding the *beurre manié* in small pieces and heating gently.

Taste and adjust seasoning if necessary and bring to the boil. Spoon the sauce over the waiting pheasant and sprinkle with chopped parsley. Garnish with fresh bay leaves and orange slices. (Serves 6)

*R*OAST PHEASANT WITH ROWAN JELLY

Beatrix Potter and Willie Heelis were married in the autumn of 1913 in Kensington, London; the honeymoon was spent at Sawrey.
Willie was a keen sportsman and there was nothing he liked better than a good day's shooting. He went rough shooting with members of the country set whom he met in the course of his work as a solicitor in Hawkshead, and was considered by the locals to be 'a great man wi' a gun.'
Beatrix did not share Willie's interest in field sports, although I am sure she must have enjoyed eating the game shot by her husband.

2 oven-ready, large fresh cock pheasants
2 thinly pared strips of lemon rind
12 sprigs of fresh parsley
12 sprigs of fresh thyme
Softened butter
Salt and freshly milled black pepper
4–5 (6 US) tablespoons rowan jelly (see page 159)
600 ml (1 pint/2½ cups) stock, made from the
pheasant giblets
Juice of ½ lemon
Sprigs of fresh thyme, to garnish
Small clusters of rowan berries, to garnish

Pre-heat the oven to 230°C (450°F, gas mark 8).

Wipe the birds inside and out with absorbent kitchen paper. Put a strip of lemon rind and 1 sprig of each of the herbs into the body cavity of the birds, plus a little butter. Add extra softened butter to the breasts and place in a roasting tin, then cover the birds with the remaining herbs and season with salt and pepper. Cook in a hot oven for 10 minutes, then reduce the temperature to 200°C (400°F, gas mark 6), and cook for a further 50 minutes. Fifteen minutes before the pheasants are cooked, remove from the oven and discard the herbs. Spread each bird with about 2 (3 US) tablespoons of rowan jelly, then return to the oven for the skin to crisp.

Take out the pheasants, place them on a warm serving dish and keep them warm while you make the sauce. Put the roasting tin on top of the stove, over moderate heat. Pour in the stock and add the remaining rowan jelly and lemon juice. Bring to the boil, stirring in any residue from the bottom of the pan. Simmer the sauce until it is reduced by half, remove any fat from the surface, then taste and adjust seasoning as necessary. (Add a little more lemon juice if it is too sweet.)

Carve or joint the birds and serve with the sauce. Garnish with fresh thyme and rowan berries. (Serves 6)

EES WYKE PARTRIDGE

Lakefield, later renamed Ees Wyke (house on the shore), is a large Georgian country house in Sawrey and was one of the Potters' most popular holiday homes. It is now a very comfortable hotel run by John and Margaret Williams. The guests are provided with enormous traditional Lakeland breakfasts and delicious dinners. This recipe is one of John's specialities. Pigeon, pheasant or chicken may be cooked in the same way.

6 oven-ready partridge
25 g (1 oz/2 US tablespoons) butter
Salt and freshly-milled black pepper

For the stock

1 medium carrot, chopped
1 medium onion, including the skin, quartered
1 celery stick, chopped
1 small piece of swede or turnip, chopped
1 bay leaf
6 whole black peppercorns
A few parsley stalks
2–3 blades of mace
Sprig of fresh thyme or 2 pinches of dried

For the sauce

25 g (1 oz) green peppercorns
175 g (6 oz) fresh strawberries
40 g (1½ oz/3 US tablespoons) butter
40 g (1½ oz/⅓ cup) plain flour
2–4 (3–5 US) tablespoons double cream
Salt and freshly milled black pepper

To make the stock, cut off the legs from the birds and place them in a large saucepan. Cover with cold water, then add the vegetables, herbs and flavouring. Bring to the boil, then almost cover with a lid and simmer gently for about 2 hours.

Strain the stock, cool it and remove the fat from the surface before using.

Pre-heat the oven to 230°C (450°F, gas mark 6).

Place the remaining partridge breasts (on the bone) on a buttered baking tray. Season with salt and black pepper, then roast in the pre-heated oven for 10–20 minutes, depending on how pink you like your partridge. (The important thing is not to dry out the breasts.) Remove from the oven and leave to relax in a warm place for a further 10 minutes.

Meanwhile, to make the sauce, place the stock in a saucepan with the green peppercorns. Chop the strawberries, reserving a few whole berries for garnish, and add to the stock. Bring to the boil, then reduce to about 300 ml (½ pint). Make *beurre manié* by beating the butter and flour together, and add it in small pieces to the sauce until the sauce has thickened to a coating consistency. Stir in the double cream. Taste and season as necessary.

Remove the breasts from the carcases and cut into slices with a sharp knife. Arrange in a fan shape on 6 warm dinner plates and place under a hot grill for a few seconds only. Carefully coat the partridge with the sauce and garnish with reserved strawberries.

Serve immediately with fresh green vegetables or a green salad. (Serves 6)

PIGEONS IN A POT WITH RED CABBAGE AND DAMSONS

6 young oven-ready pigeons
6 sprigs of fresh thyme
6 sprigs of fresh parsley
40 g (1½ oz/3 tablespoons) butter
1½ (2 US) tablespoons sunflower oil
1 tablespoon seasoned plain wholemeal flour
1 large onion, sliced
1 small red cabbage, finely shredded
3 whole cloves
150 ml (¼ pint/⅔ cup) elderberry wine or port
250 g (8 oz) damsons or small purple plums, stoned and halved
Salt and freshly milled black pepper
Freshly grated nutmeg
Chopped fresh thyme or parsley, to garnish

Pre-heat the oven to 170°C (325°F, gas mark 3).

Wipe the pigeons inside and out with absorbent kitchen paper and put a sprig of thyme and parsley inside each one. Heat the butter and oil in a large frying pan. Coat the pigeons lightly in the flour, then add to the pan and fry, turning occasionally, until browned all over. Transfer with a slotted spoon to an ovenproof casserole dish.

Add the onion to the frying pan and cook for about 5 minutes until soft, then stir in the cabbage. Cook for a few minutes, then add the cloves and the elderberry wine or port. Bring to the boil, then spoon over the pigeons. Arrange the halved damsons or plums over the top. Cover tightly and bake in a slow oven for 1½ hours, or until the pigeons are tender.

Transfer the pigeons, vegetables and fruit to a warmed serving platter, using a slotted spoon. Boil the cooking liquor for 2–3 minutes to thicken and concentrate the flavour. Season to taste as necessary with salt, pepper and nutmeg, then pour over the pigeons. Serve immediately, sprinkled with chopped thyme or parsley. (Serves 6)

BEEFSTEAK, PIGEON AND MUSHROOM PUDDING

Beatrix once complained about having to illustrate 'namby pamby pigeons'. Perhaps she preferred pigeons in a casserole or a pudding, like those that Willie shot!

For the filling

3 oven-ready pigeons
Cold water to cover
1 small carrot, chopped
1 small onion stuck with 2 whole cloves, plus the onion skin
1 stick of celery, chopped
1 bay leaf
6 whole black peppercorns
450 g (1 lb) braising steak (boneless beef round), cubed

1 tablespoon seasoned plain wholemeal flour
350 g (12 oz) field mushrooms, or large cultivated mushrooms
1 tablespoon sunflower or safflower oil
1 tablespoon elderberry wine or port

For the suet crust

350 g (12 oz/2½ cups) self-raising flour
1 teaspoon salt
Freshly milled black pepper
1 teaspoon dried thyme
175 g (6 oz) shredded suet
About 175 ml (6 fl oz/¾ cup) cold water, to mix

Cut off the breasts from the pigeons, removing the skin, and dice the breast meat. Put the pigeon carcasses in a large saucepan and cover with water. Add the vegetables, bay leaf and peppercorns, then bring to the boil. Simmer until reduced to 300 ml (½ pint/1¼ cups). Roll the beef in seasoned flour and slice the mushrooms fairly thickly. Fry the beef quickly in the oil for a few minutes to brown it all over.

To make the suet crust, sieve the flour and salt together into a mixing bowl. Season with pepper and stir in the thyme and suet. Mix with as much water as necessary to make a soft dough. Knead lightly, then roll out on a lightly floured surface to about 6 mm (¼ in) thick. Use three-quarters of the pastry to line a well-buttered 1.5-litre (2½-pint/1½-quart US) pudding basin.

Pack the pigeon, beef and mushrooms into the basin and pour in the reduced stock and the elderberry wine or port. Roll out the remaining pastry to make a lid for the basin. Brush the top edge of the crust with a little milk and put on the lid, pinching the edges together to seal them. Cover the pudding with a double layer of buttered and pleated greaseproof paper and foil. Tie securely under the basin rim with string. Steam for 4½–5 hours, topping up with boiling water as necessary.

To serve, wrap the outside of the basin in a clean cloth. Accompany with a green vegetable. (Serves 6)

CASSEROLE OF VENISON WITH JUNIPER BERRIES

While the Potter men and their friends stalked deer to shoot during summer holidays in Scotland, Beatrix tracked the shy roe-deer to study them in their natural state: 'Finding this deer-stalking a pleasing excitement,' she writes in her journal in October, 1892. 'I trudged up the road with the hand camera, in hopes of getting a pretty roe-deer.'
When you cook this dish (which comes from the Mill Hotel in Mungrisdale, Lakeland, and is pictured there, right), allow time for marinating, preferably overnight. I also find that cooking the casserole one day and reheating the next gives the best results.

1.5 kg (3 lb) shoulder of venison
350 ml (12 fl oz/1½ cups) dry white wine
125 g (4 oz/¾ cup) seasoned flour
50 g (2 oz/¼ cup) butter
2 (3 US) tablespoons sunflower oil
Beef stock
Salt and freshly milled black pepper
10 juniper berries, crushed
1½ teaspoons tomato purée
1 bouquet garni
350 g (12 oz) wild mushrooms
1 bunch spring onions
Chopped fresh parsley, to garnish

Cut the venison into 5-cm (2-in) chunks, trimming away any tough membrane or sinew. Place in a dish and pour over the wine. Cover and leave to marinate in a cool place for several hours, or overnight, stirring from time to time.

Pre-heat the oven to 170°C (325°F, gas mark 3).

Drain off the wine and reserve, then dry the meat well with absorbent kitchen paper and toss in seasoned flour. Heat the butter and oil in a large frying pan and fry the meat, a little at a time, for about 10 minutes, until well browned on all sides. Using a slotted spoon, transfer to an ovenproof casserole dish. Stir any remaining flour into the fat in the frying pan and cook gently, stirring, until brown.

Remove the pan from the heat and gradually stir in the reserved wine. Pour over the meat and add enough beef stock barely to cover it. Stir well, then season to taste and add the crushed juniper berries, tomato purée and the bouquet garni. Cover the casserole and cook in a slow oven for 1½–2 hours, or until the meat is tender.

Thickly slice the mushrooms and finely chop the spring onions. Remove the casserole dish from the oven and add these vegetables. Put back into the oven for a further 20–30 minutes until the vegetables are tender.

Remove the casserole from the oven and skim off any fat. Discard the bouquet garni and taste. Adjust the seasoning as necessary, then garnish with chopped parsley.

Serve with bread or jacket potatoes and rowan jelly (see page 159). (Serves 6)

HUNTSMAN'S POT

This recipe, kindly given to me by Jean Butterworth from Grasmere, is a marvellous dish for a winter party.

1 oven-ready pheasant
1 rabbit, cleaned
450 g (1 lb) venison, cubed
6 juniper berries, crushed
1 bay leaf, crushed
300 ml (½ pint/1¼ cups) olive oil
600 ml (1 pint/2½ cups) red wine
2 large onions, sliced
2–3 (3–4 US) tablespoons plain flour
2 large cloves of garlic, crushed
2 (3 US) tablespoons tomato purée
1 bouquet garni
600 ml (1 pint/2½ cups) game or beef stock
Salt and freshly milled black pepper
450 g (1 lb) braising steak (boneless beef round), cubed
2 (3 US) tablespoons redcurrant jelly
Chopped fresh parsley, to garnish

In this recipe a mixture of game is first marinated for 24 hours, then casseroled in a slow oven. Any combination of game works well.

Cut the pheasant and rabbit in half and place in a large bowl with the venison. Mix the crushed juniper berries, crushed bay leaf, oil and red wine together, then pour over the game. Leave in a cool place for 24 hours, or at least overnight, turning from time to time.

Pre-heat the oven to 170°C (325°F, gas mark 3).

Drain off and reserve the marinade. Heat a little of the oil from the marinade in a frying pan and fry the onions for about 10 minutes until soft and lightly browned. Stir in the flour and cook, stirring, until a rich brown. Remove from the heat, leave to cool a little, then stir in the remaining marinade. Put back on the heat and bring to the boil. Simmer for a few minutes, then add the garlic, tomato purée, bouquet garni and stock. Season well, then bring back to the boil.

Put the venison and beef in a large ovenproof casserole dish and lay the pheasant and rabbit on top. Pour over the sauce and cook in a slow oven for about 2½ hours, or until very tender. Remove any fat on top of the casserole with absorbent kitchen paper and discard the bouquet garni.

Lift out the pheasant and rabbit with a slotted spoon and cut all the meat off the bone. Discard the bones and cut the meat into chunks. Return the meat to the casserole with the redcurrant jelly. Taste and adjust seasoning as necessary, reheat gently, then sprinkle with chopped parsley. Serve with warm herb soda bread or scones (see pages 124 and 131) to mop up the gravy, and pickled damsons (see page 164). (Serves 6–8)

RABBIT CASSEROLE WITH CHEESE AND HERB DUMPLINGS

Rabbits were always part of Beatrix Potter's life, as pets and also as models for her sketches and paintings; but she must have put many wild ones in a pot as her husband Willie was such a good shot!

175 g (6 oz) green streaky bacon rashers, de-rinded
Selected rabbit joints, total weight about 1 kg (2½ lb)
2 leeks, sliced
2 parsnips, chopped
4 carrots, sliced
4 sticks of celery, chopped
3 tablespoons (¼ cup) plain flour
300 ml (½ pint/1¼ cups) still dry cider
600 ml (1 pint/2½ cups) chicken stock
Salt and freshly milled black pepper
1 bay leaf
Sprig of fresh lavender, thyme or rosemary
Sprigs of fresh lavender and marigold petals,
to garnish

For the dumplings

125 g (4 oz/¾ cup) self-raising flour
Pinch of salt
Freshly milled black pepper
½ teaspoon dried thyme
1 teaspoon chopped fresh parsley
1 tablespoon chopped fresh chives
50 g (2 oz/½ cup) shredded suet
50 g (2 oz/½ cup) mature Cheddar cheese,
finely grated

Pre-heat the oven to 170°C (325°F, gas mark 3).

Chop the bacon and fry gently in a flameproof casserole dish until the fat runs. Wash and dry the rabbit joints, then add them to the casserole and fry gently until browned all over. Remove them with a slotted spoon and place on a plate while you fry the vegetables, adding a little butter if necessary. Sprinkle in the flour and stir well. Cook for 1–2 minutes, then remove from the heat and gradually add the cider and the stock. Bring to the boil, stirring continuously, then season to taste. Add the herbs, and the rabbit, and cover and bake in a slow oven for about 1½ hours, or until the rabbit is tender.

To make the dumplings, sieve the flour and salt together into a bowl. Season with pepper and stir in the thyme, parsley, chives, suet and grated cheese. Add enough cold water to mix to a soft dough. Shape into 12 small balls.

Twenty minutes before the end of the cooking time, taste and adjust the seasoning if necessary. Place the dumplings on top of the casserole, then cover again and bake for 20 minutes until they are well risen. Remove the lid and brown under a hot grill for a few minutes, if you like crispy dumplings.

Serve immediately, garnished with a few tiny sprigs of lavender and sprinkled with marigold petals. (Serves 6)

OLD ENGLISH RABBIT PIE

Leg fillets or shoulder joints are good for this dish – use wild or fresh farmed English rabbit.

Selected rabbit joints, total weight about 1 kg (2½ lb)
2 onions, finely sliced
1 medium cooking apple, peeled and sliced
250 g (8 oz) green streaky bacon, in one piece
1 bay leaf
½ teaspoon dried thyme or 1½ teaspoons chopped
fresh thyme
Salt and freshly milled black pepper
300 ml (½ pint/1¼ cups) still dry cider
450 ml (¾ pint/scant 2 cups) chicken stock
125 g (4 oz) prunes, stoned
40 g (1½ oz/3 US tablespoons) butter
40 g (1½ oz/⅓ cup) plain wholemeal flour
1 teaspoon freshly grated nutmeg
250 g (8 oz) puff pastry
1 egg, beaten, to glaze
150 ml (¼ pint/⅔ cup) soured cream, to finish

Wipe the rabbit joints with absorbent kitchen paper and place them in a large saucepan. Add the onion and apple. Chop the bacon into 2.5-cm (1-in) cubes and add to the pan with the bay leaf and thyme. Season well, then pour on the cider and stock. Heat to simmering point, skim if necessary, then cover and simmer gently for about 1 hour, or until the rabbit is tender.

Using a slotted spoon, transfer the rabbit, bacon, apple and onion to a 1.5-litre (2½-pint/1½-quart US) pie dish. Chop the prunes and sprinkle over the rabbit. Beat the butter and flour together and add in small pieces to the stock in the saucepan. Heat gently to thicken, then taste and adjust seasoning with salt, pepper and nutmeg. Bring to simmering point, then pour over the rabbit. Leave to cool.

Pre-heat the oven to 220°C (425°F, gas mark 5).

When the filling is cool, roll out the pastry on a lightly floured surface, so that it is at least 2.5 cm (1 in) wider than the top of the pie dish. Cut off a strip 2.5 cm (1 in) wide and fit on to the dampened rim of the dish. Press this down firmly. Brush the pastry rim with beaten egg glaze and place the pastry lid on top, pressing down well all round to seal the edges. Trim and flute the edges, then roll out the trimmings and use to cut into leaves and other shapes, to decorate. Make a small hole for the steam to escape, then brush the top of the pie with beaten egg. Stand the pie on a baking sheet and bake in the centre of a hot oven for about 20 minutes, until a light golden brown. Reduce the temperature to 190°C (375°F, gas mark 5) and bake for a further 20 minutes, or until well browned and crisp. (Cover with foil if the pastry is browning too much.)

Remove from the oven and pour the soured cream into the pie through the hole in the top. Shake the dish to distribute the cream, and serve with mashed or plain boiled potatoes and a green vegetable or salad. (Serves 6)

Variations

Substitute chicken joints for the rabbit in both the previous recipes and make as before.

EGGS AND CHEESE

CHANTERELLE SCRAMBLE

Beatrix Potter's interest in fungi and lichen began while the family was holidaying at Dunkeld in Perthshire, and she might well have devoted her life to fungi if she had had any professional encouragement. Only in recent years has it come to light just how extensively she studied the subject; she made over three hundred drawings of fungi and formulated various theories, especially about the germination of spores.

Chanterelles can be found from late June to October in established woodlands where there is a mixture of deciduous (especially beech) and conifer trees, and where the ground is covered with bracken. Once you have found them, return to the same spot every year, for they are sure to be there – while the wood is, anyway. Cut them from the ground near the base of their stems. Any other mushrooms, preferably wild, can be used in this recipe, but chanterelles go superbly with eggs because of their lovely yellow colour. (Take care, however, not to experiment with wild mushrooms unless you are absolutely sure they are an edible variety!)

250–300 g (8–10 oz) chanterelle mushrooms
50 g (2 oz/¼ cup) butter
12 large eggs
Salt and freshly milled black pepper

Wipe the mushrooms and check that they are insect-free at the top of the stems (although one of the good things about chanterelles is that they are seldom attacked by creepy-crawlies). Thinly slice the mushrooms, but don't peel them.

Melt the butter in a heavy pan and cook the mushrooms gently for about 10 minutes, stirring occasionally. Drain off any excess moisture. Beat the eggs with a little salt and plenty of pepper, then stir them into the mushrooms. Keep stirring over a low heat until the eggs are thick and creamy. Serve immediately with chunks of warm crusty wholemeal bread or new potatoes, and a crisp salad. (Serves 6)

EGGY BREAD WITH DAMSON CHUTNEY

One of the greatest admirers of Beatrix Potter's early work was her uncle, Sir Henry Roscoe, Vice-Chancellor of London University. The Roscoes lived in a large house with grounds at Woodcote in Surrey; Beatrix spent several Christmases there, and became friendly with the Roscoes' youngest daughter, Dora, who shared her interest in painting.

To celebrate publication of the textbook written by her uncle and a colleague, Joseph Lunt, First Step in Chemistry, *Beatrix gave him a drawing entitled 'A Dream of Toasted Cheese', with a caption which jokingly alluded to a statement in the book on ammonia gas, 'The peculiar pungent smell of this compound is noticed if we heat a bit of CHEESE in a test-tube'!*

450 ml (¾ pint/scant 2 cups) milk
6 small eggs
12 slices wholemeal bread
175 g (6 oz/¾ cup) butter
A little sunflower oil
700 g (1½ lb) Cheshire or Lancashire cheese, grated
About 6 pickled onions, chopped
About 4 tablespoons (⅓ cup) damson chutney or any fruit-based chutney (see also page 165)
Sunflower seeds

Beat together the milk and the eggs. Dip the slices of bread in the egg mixture and leave to soak until it is all absorbed. Melt some of the butter with a little oil in a large frying pan and fry the soaked bread, several slices at a time, until golden brown on both sides, adding more butter as necessary. Keep warm.

Mix together the cheese and chopped pickled onions. Spread a little chutney over the eggy bread, followed by the cheese mixture. Sprinkle with sunflower seeds, then cook briefly under a medium-hot grill until the seeds are toasted and the cheese is golden brown and bubbling. Serve immediately with a large crisp salad, or on its own. (Serves 6)

*H*AZELNUT, CHEESE AND VEGETABLE BAKE

During a stay at Lingholm, a large country house on Derwentwater, in 1901, Beatrix Potter wrote the complete story of Squirrel Nutkin in a letter to Norah Moore, one of the children of her former governess. The squirrels sail over the water to Owl Island to gather nuts. Hazelnuts can be collected in late September from woods and hedgerows to make the most nutritious meals. Amazingly enough, weight for weight, they contain 50 per cent more protein, seven times more fat and five times more carbohydrate than hen eggs. No wonder the squirrels love them!

For the base

250 g (8 oz/2½ cups) fresh wholemeal breadcrumbs
75 g (3 oz/6 US tablespoons) butter or margarine
175 g (6 oz/1½ cups) grated Cheddar cheese
175 g (6 oz/1⅓ cups) finely chopped hazelnuts
1 tablespoon chopped fresh thyme or 1 teaspoon dried
2 large cloves of garlic, crushed
Salt and freshly milled black pepper

For the filling

75 g (3 oz/6 US tablespoons) butter
4 medium leeks, sliced
40 g (1½ oz/⅓ cup) plain flour
450 ml (¾ pint/scant 2 cups) milk
6 medium tomatoes, skinned and chopped
Salt and freshly milled black pepper
Freshly grated nutmeg
40 g (1½ oz/½ cup) fresh wholemeal breadcrumbs
125 g (4 oz/1 cup) grated Cheddar cheese

Pre-heat the oven to 220°C (425°F, gas mark 7).

To make the base, place the breadcrumbs in a mixing bowl and rub in the butter. Stir in the other ingredients, then press the mixture into a greased roasting tin or ovenproof dish, 30 by 20 cm (12 by 8 in). Bake in a hot oven for 15–20 minutes, or until golden brown.

To make the topping, melt the butter in a large saucepan. Fry the leeks gently for about 5 minutes until soft, then stir in the flour. Cook for 1–2 minutes, then gradually stir in the milk. Cook very gently until thick, and bring to the boil. Reduce the heat and add the chopped tomatoes. Simmer for a few minutes to soften the tomatoes, then season well with salt, pepper and nutmeg. Spoon the vegetable mixture over the cooked base and sprinkle with the breadcrumbs mixed with the cheese. Cook in a moderate oven (180°C, 350°F, gas mark 4) for 20–30 minutes until the cheese has melted and is golden brown.

Serve at once with a crisp green salad. (Serves 6)

GLOUCESTER CHEESE STEW

Beatrix formed a lifelong friendship with her cousin, Caroline Hutton, who later became a farmer after her marriage, just as Beatrix did. She first stayed with Caroline at her home, Harescombe Grange, near Stroud in Gloucestershire, when she was 27, and was immediately impressed by her independent cousin. 'I travelled with her from Paddington . . . We ranged over universal subjects and became indiscreet before reaching Swindon, also very hoarse, and had several flat differences of opinion.'
This visit was the first of many, and on one occasion Caroline told Beatrix the intriguing story of the Tailor of Gloucester, whose work was magically finished by unseen hands. Beatrix adapted it as one of the 'little books' — her own favourite — and made several sketches of the city on excursions from Harescombe Grange.

900 g (2 lb) potatoes
600 ml (1 pint/2½ cups) creamy milk
Salt and freshly milled black pepper
Freshly grated nutmeg
3 medium onions or 2 large cloves of garlic
350 g (12 oz/3 cups) grated Double Gloucester cheese
Chopped fresh parsley

Pre-heat the oven to 180°C (350°F, gas mark 4).

Peel the potatoes and slice thinly. Put them in a saucepan with the milk. Season well with salt, pepper and nutmeg, then simmer gently for 15 minutes until almost tender, but not broken up. Using a slotted spoon, remove the potatoes from the milk, reserving the milk on one side. Chop the onions or garlic finely.

Butter an ovenproof casserole dish and arrange layers of potato, onion or garlic and cheese in it, seasoning well between each layer and ending with a layer of cheese. Pour over the reserved milk and bake uncovered in a moderate oven for about 1 hour, or until most of the liquid has been absorbed and the top is golden brown. Sprinkle with parsley and serve with a green salad for supper or lunch, or in smaller portions to accompany meat, fish or poultry. (Serves 6)

SUFFOLK HAM TOASTS

Beatrix Potter often went to stay with her cousin, Lady Ethel Hyde Parker, at Melford Hall in Suffolk. The squirrels there inspired her to plan out The Tale of Squirrel Nutkin, *on a visit in 1903. She was also working on* The Tailor of Gloucester *at that time, and wrote to her editor, Norman Warne, from Melford Hall, 'I have been able to draw an oldfashioned fireplace here, very suitable for the tailor's kitchen.' Beatrix painted several other views in the grounds of this lovely house. Perhaps ham featured on the menu, for ham and bacon curing is a traditional East Anglian industry. Suffolk sweet-cured hams are renowned, although rarer today than they were in Beatrix's day. They take nearly ten weeks to cure and are smoked over an applewood and oak fire to develop their characteristic shiny black skins.*

350 g (12 oz) good quality lean ham
6 thick slices of wholemeal bread
125 g (4 oz/½ cup) unsalted butter
2 (3 US) tablespoons double cream or crème fraîche
Salt and freshly milled black pepper
12 large eggs
Chopped fresh chives, to garnish

Finely chop or mince the ham. Toast the bread, then butter each slice, using about half the butter in total. Keep warm in a very low oven. Put the cream in a saucepan, stir in the ham and season with plenty of black pepper. Heat very gently until warmed through, then spread over the hot buttered toast and return to the oven to keep warm.

Beat the eggs well with a fork and season to taste. Melt the remaining butter in a saucepan and stir in the beaten eggs. Continue to cook, stirring all the time, until the eggs are just on the point of setting. Quickly spoon the scrambled egg on to the ham toasts and serve immediately, garnished with chopped chives. (Serves 6)

Gloucester cheese stew (above right) with a cream cheese, onion and walnut tart

CREAM CHEESE, ONION AND WALNUT TART

For her fourth book Beatrix Potter wrote a sequel to The Tale of Peter Rabbit, *this time featuring Peter's bold cousin, Benjamin Bunny. Once again the story takes place in Mr McGregor's garden, and Beatrix made many sketches of the kitchen garden at Fawe Park on Derwentwater, where the family was spending the summer of 1903. These views appear as backgrounds in the book and, although Fawe Park is not open to the public, the gardens have been very little changed to this day.*

Beatrix obviously enjoyed painting the backgrounds for The Tale of Benjamin Bunny *and there are no fewer than three of her beautifully painted studies of onions for the book in the Victoria and Albert Museum.*

For the pastry

75 g (3 oz/½ cup) self-raising flour
75 g (3 oz/½ cup) wholemeal plain flour
Large pinch of salt
1 teaspoon dry mustard
110 g (4 oz/½ cup) butter or hard margarine
50 g (2 oz/½ cup) grated Cheddar cheese
1 large egg yolk
1–2 (1½–3 US) tablespoons cold water

For the filling

40 g (1½ oz/3 US tablespoons) butter
450 g (1 lb) large onions, thinly sliced
1 large clove of garlic, crushed
½ teaspoon soft brown sugar
1½ (2 US) tablespoons chopped fresh basil or 1½ teaspoons dried basil
75 g (3 oz/¾ cup) chopped walnuts or hazelnuts
125 g (4 oz) cream cheese, or other soft cheese
300 ml (½ pint/1¼ cups) single cream or milk
2 large eggs
Salt and freshly milled black pepper
Large pinch of freshly grated nutmeg
Sprigs of fresh basil and chive flowers, to garnish

To make the pastry, sieve the flours together with the salt and mustard into a large mixing bowl. Cut the fat into small pieces and work into the flour with a palette knife until well-coated, then rub in with the fingertips until the mixture resembles breadcrumbs. Stir in the grated cheese. Beat the egg yolk lightly with the water, then mix quickly into the fat and flour, using a palette knife, to make a firm dough. Turn on to a lightly floured surface and knead lightly until smooth. Wrap in a polythene bag and chill in the fridge for about 30 minutes. Roll out the pastry and use to line a lightly greased 22.5-cm (9-in) loose-bottomed fluted flan tin. Chill in the fridge for a further 30 minutes.

Meanwhile, make the filling. Melt the butter in a frying pan and fry the onions very gently until they turn pale golden. Add the garlic, sugar and basil and continue cooking until the onions turn slightly browner in colour. Stir in the nuts and spoon the mixture into the prepared pastry case. Dot with small pieces of cream cheese. Beat the cream or milk and eggs together and season well with salt, pepper and nutmeg to taste. Pour over the onions.

Pre-heat the oven to 190°C (375°F, gas mark 5), with a baking tray inside.

Place the flan on the hot baking tray and bake in a fairly hot oven for 35–40 minutes, or until the filling is puffed and set and a rich golden brown. Garnish the tart with basil and chive flowers and serve warm for lunch or supper with a crisp green or tomato salad. (Serves 6)

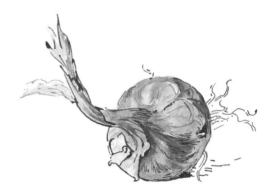

BABY WELSH EGGS

North Wales was another area of the country where Beatrix Potter often stayed. She frequently visited Gwaynynog, the house of her uncle Fred Burton. Beatrix may have tasted Glamorgan sausagemeat during these visits. It is a traditional and delicious savoury meatless mixture, originally named after the hard, white cheese from Glamorgan which is made from the milk of a rare breed of white cattle known as 'Glamorgan Cattle'. Here, it is wrapped around tiny bantam or quail eggs. These eggs will appeal especially to children or elderly people, who might find a large egg just too much. Tiny Scotch eggs, made with pork sausagemeat, also look very pretty and are easy to handle.

275 g (9 oz/2 cups) fine wholemeal breadcrumbs
40 g (1½ oz/2 US tablespoons) finely chopped green part of leek or spring onion
5 tablespoons (⅓ cup) finely chopped fresh parsley
4 tablespoons (¼ cup) finely chopped very young nettles (optional)
2 teaspoons finely chopped fresh lemon thyme
175 g (6 oz/1½ cups) grated Caerphilly or other good quality hard cheese
Large pinch of salt and freshly milled black pepper
1 teaspoon mustard powder
3 standard (medium) eggs
12 bantam or quail eggs
Sunflower or safflower oil, for frying

Mix 150 g (5 oz/1¼ cups) of the breadcrumbs with the chopped leek or spring onion, parsley, nettles (if using), lemon thyme and cheese. Season well with salt, black pepper and mustard. Beat 1 whole medium egg and 2 medium egg yolks lightly together, then mix into the breadcrumb and cheese mixture to bind together. Leave on one side for about 1 hour to allow the flavours to blend.

Meanwhile, hard-boil the little eggs for about 8 minutes. Cool in cold water, then shell carefully.

Divide the savoury cheese mixture into 12 portions. Flatten each portion into a circle and wrap firmly and evenly round each egg, making sure there are no cracks. (Use the palm of one hand to cup the savoury coating and egg, while you work the mixture round the egg with the other hand.)

Beat the 2 egg whites lightly with a fork. Dip each coated egg into the egg whites, then roll them in the remaining breadcrumbs until evenly coated. Chill for about 20 minutes to firm up.

Fry in deep fat at 180°C (350°F) for about 4 minutes, or until golden brown and cooked right through. Drain well on absorbent kitchen paper and serve piping hot with a green salad for lunch or supper. The eggs are also excellent when cold for picnics and packed lunches. (Makes about 12)

Variation

GLAMORGAN SAUSAGES

Mix the savoury cheese mixture as before, then divide into small sausages. Roll in a little seasoned flour, then dip into the lightly beaten egg white. Roll in breadcrumbs and shallow fry in lard or oil. Serve with creamed potatoes or chips and home-made tomato sauce or red tomato chutney.

DECORATED PACE EGGS

'Pace' comes from the old English 'pasch', meaning Easter, and pace eggs are eggs specially decorated for the festival. Decorating eggs in this way is a centuries-old custom, once common in the North; the Wordsworth Museum at Grasmere houses a collection of highly ornate eggs, originally made for the poet's children.

Pace eggs were hard-boiled and dyed various colours, usually with flowers and plants; Kendal, however, was once a great centre for cotton weaving and Groves Bros, the dyers, used to leave out vats of dye for the children to help themselves. More elaborate effects were achieved by wrapping flowers and ferns round the egg before dying and names and sentiments were sometimes printed on the eggs. They were given to friends and neighbours who ate them for breakfast on Easter Sunday, kept them as ornaments or used them for games like 'pace egg rolling'. Beatrix Potter used to decorate pace eggs for the local children of Sawrey to use in their egg-rolling races on Easter Monday. Popular entertainers in Near Sawrey on Easter Saturday were the 'Jolly Boys', or 'Pace Eggers', who performed the old pace-egg mummer's play which included the characters of Lord Nelson, the Doctor, Bessy Brown Bags and Tosspot.

Mollie Green, who still serves teas in her cottage at Sawrey, had two brothers, Harry and Jack, who were in the group – she was allowed to join as 'Mollie Mascot'. They called at houses in the village, acted their parts and sang a traditional song; a basket was then held out to

receive offerings of pennies and pace eggs. Beatrix and Willie always gave a warm welcome to the Jolly Boys when they called at Castle Cottage. Willow Taylor, who lived at the Tower Bank Arms in Beatrix's time, told me that this Easter (1990), a group of folk-dancers from Millom performed the traditional Jolly Boy play outside the pub. Mollie Green was there – and she approved of their effort! You can of course make decorated eggs by painting designs directly on to the shells with water-colour paint. (If necessary mix with a very tiny drop of washing-up liquid to help the paint adhere to the shell.) The following recipe demonstrates the traditional method of using natural products to dye and pattern the eggs.

Below: delicate fern dyes and lively paintings on pace eggs

Primroses, primulas and pieces of fern
6 smooth-shelled large white or pale brown eggs
Onion skins
2.5-cm (1-in) wide bandage
12 elastic bands

Holding the flowers and ferns by the stem, dip them one at a time very briefly into boiling water to soften them enough to stick to the eggs. Arrange a few immediately on the surface of an unboiled egg to form a very simple pattern. Hold the flowers in position, cover the egg with onion skins and, while holding firmly, bandage up tightly. Keep everything in place with 2 elastic bands. Repeat the whole process with the 5 other eggs.

Place the eggs carefully in a saucepan of cold water and bring gently to the boil, then simmer for about 15 minutes. Cool in cold water and peel off the bandage. The dyed eggs may then be washed before serving. Arrange in a basket lined with moss, straw or feathers to look like a nest.

Another attractive effect can be produced by placing dark red primulas, that have been briefly dipped in boiling water, on an unboiled egg. Wrap tightly with bandage and boil as before. The flowers will leave a pale grey imprint on the eggs.

DUCK EGG GRATIN WITH ARTICHOKES AND LEEKS

Beatrix Potter's ducks at Hill Top Farm were the models for her story, The Tale of Jemima Puddle-Duck. *Hill Top was Beatrix Potter's first property, purchased with the royalties from her 'little books' and a small legacy. The farm was managed by John Cannon and his wife and Beatrix asked them to stay on, as she was new to farming and still officially living at home with her parents.*

She built new rooms on to the side of the house for the Cannons and their two children, Ralph and Betsy, and later dedicated The Tale of Jemima Puddle-Duck *to them, 'A farmyard tale for Ralph and Betsy'. Their mother can be seen feeding the poultry in one picture (see below), and the children are taking away Jemima's eggs in another.*

450 g (1 lb) Jerusalem artichokes
6 duck or large hen eggs
700 g (1½ lb) leeks, when prepared
125 g (4 oz/½ cup) butter
2 (3 US) tablespoons plain flour
600 ml (1 pint/2½ cups) milk
150 g (5 oz/1¼ cups) grated Gruyère cheese
125 g (4 oz/1 cup) grated Cheddar cheese
Salt and freshly milled black pepper
Freshly grated nutmeg
2 large cloves of garlic, crushed
French bread, sliced

Pre-heat the oven to 200°C (400°F, gas mark 6).

Scrub the artichokes and simmer in boiling salted water for 10–15 minutes, or until just tender. Drain the artichokes well, reserving the cooking liquor for soup, and run under a cold tap to cool. Skin them when cool enough to handle, slice thickly and arrange in a layer in the bottom of a large, buttered gratin or baking dish. Meanwhile, boil the eggs for about 10 minutes.

Trim, wash and thinly slice the leeks. Melt half the butter in a large saucepan and cook the leeks gently for a few minutes until tender, stirring to coat them with butter. Remove the pan from the heat and add the flour. Gradually add the milk, stirring constantly. Return to the heat and cook until you have a smooth, thick sauce. Allow to simmer for a few minutes while you shell the eggs. Halve or quarter them and arrange on top of the artichokes.

Stir just over half the Gruyère and all the Cheddar cheese into the sauce and season with salt and plenty of black pepper and nutmeg. Pour the sauce over the eggs and artichokes.

Place the crushed garlic with the remaining butter in a large frying pan. Melt the butter and fry the slices of French bread very lightly in it, on one side only. Arrange the bread on top of the dish, garlic-buttered side up. Scatter with the remaining cheese – just a little over the bread and more generously between the slices. Bake in a fairly hot oven for about 30 minutes, or until the crust is crisp and golden brown. (Serves 6)

ℒITTLE PIG ROBINSON'S SPRING CAULIFLOWER CHEESE

The Tale of Little Pig Robinson was published in 1930, and was the last of the Peter Rabbit books to appear. It is a long and adventurous story about an innocent young pig who is kidnapped by a ship's cook while shopping at the local market. Little Pig Robinson was sent on his ill-fated expedition to Stymouth by his aunts Dorcas and Porcas, with a big basket containing two dozen eggs, a bunch of daffodils and two spring cauliflowers. I love these cauliflowers; they look so fresh and appetising and would make a delicious 'cheese'. This particular recipe was given to me by the late Michael Smith, a chef and cookery writer who did so much to promote the glories of traditional British food.

225 ml (7½ fl oz/scant 1 cup) single cream
2 (3 US) tablespoons grated Parmesan cheese
1 clove of garlic, crushed
½ teaspoon ground mace
1 large white cauliflower
Juice of 1 small lemon
Salt and freshly milled black pepper

Mix the cream with the cheese, garlic and mace in a bowl and leave to stand for at least 2 hours.

Wash the cauliflower and break into 2.5-cm (1-in) florets, discarding the main stem. Cook in boiling salted water with the lemon juice for a few minutes. (The cauliflower should still be crisp.) Drain well and keep on one side. Pour the cream mixture into the pan and season to taste. Add the cauliflower florets and toss and bubble over a highish heat until each floret is thoroughly coated. Serve immediately.

The cauliflower can be cooked in advance, rinsed under cold running water to cool completely and then drained well. Reheat with the cream mixture over a low heat, tossing and stirring well until piping hot. (Serves 3–6)

ℐEMIMA'S SAVOURY PICNIC OMELETTE

In The Tale of Jemima Puddle-Duck, gullible Jemima is delighted when the silver-tongued foxy gentleman, Beatrix's favourite villain, invites her to a private dinner-party. 'Not even the mention of sage and onions made her suspicious.' She really believes 'the gentleman with sandy whiskers' wants her to fetch herbs from the farm-garden to make a savoury omelette.
This particular savoury omelette is delicious for a picnic. If you are eating it as part of a meal, the quantity will serve 6, but as a main dish, only 3.

2 (3 US) tablespoons olive oil
1 large potato, peeled and diced
1 medium onion, finely chopped
1 small leek, finely chopped
1 large red pepper, deseeded and finely chopped
6 tablespoons (½ cup) fresh or frozen peas, cooked
3 goose or 6 duck or large hen eggs
Salt and freshly milled black pepper
3 tablespoons (¼ cup) chopped fresh parsley
2 (3 US) tablespoons grated Parmesan cheese

Heat the oil in a large frying pan, add the potato and cook for 8–10 minutes, stirring from time to time, until evenly browned. Stir in the onion and continue frying until soft, then add the leek and red pepper. Cook for a further 6–8 minutes, then stir in the peas.

Beat the eggs lightly with salt and pepper to taste, then mix in the parsley and cheese. Pour over the vegetables and cook over moderate heat for about 5 minutes, or until the omelette is just set on the underside, stirring once or twice to allow the egg mixture to run through the vegetables.

Flash the omelette under a moderately hot grill until lightly puffed and golden on top. Serve hot or warm, cut into wedges, with crusty bread, or with kidneys or bacon; otherwise leave to get cold, cover and keep in a cool place until needed. (Serves 3–6)

*S*TILTON AND LEEK PANCAKES

An unpublished story called 'The Solitary Mouse' includes this comment on the animals' tea-time: 'Where is the cheese? Don't tell me it has been left in the caravan. It may be vulgar to eat cheese at tea time but I have a tooth for cheese.' Vulgar or not, these toothsome cheesy pancakes make an excellent dish for lunch, high tea or supper.

For the pancakes

50 g (2 oz/⅓ cup) plain white flour
50 g (2 oz/⅓ cup) plain wholemeal flour
Pinch of salt
1 standard (medium) egg
300 ml (½ pint/1¼ cups) skimmed milk
Butter, for frying

For the filling

50 g (2 oz/¼ cup) butter
6 small leeks, finely sliced
Salt and freshly milled black pepper
Freshly grated nutmeg
300 g (10 oz/2½ cups) crumbled Stilton cheese
50 g (2 oz/⅓ cup) pumpkin seeds, toasted
50 g (2 oz/⅓ cup) sunflower seeds, toasted
Chopped fresh parsley, to garnish

Pre-heat the oven to 180°C (350°F, gas mark 4).

To make the pancakes, sieve the flours and salt together into a bowl. Make a well in the centre and add the egg. Gradually beat in half the milk until a smooth batter is formed, then beat in the remaining milk. Leave to stand for 1 hour.

Heat a little butter in a small frying pan and when smoking hot, pour in about 3 tablespoons (¼ cup) of the batter, tilting the pan to cover the base. Cook for 1–2 minutes, loosen the edges, and when the pancake

In the foreground Jemima's savoury picnic omelette, described on page 89, and, in the basket, goats' cheese in puff pastry parcels

moves freely, turn over to cook the other side. Transfer to a warm plate and keep warm while cooking the rest of the batter, stacking the cooked pancakes between sheets of greaseproof paper. (The mixture should make 12 pancakes.)

For the filling, melt the butter in a saucepan and stir in the leeks. Season well with salt, pepper and nutmeg, then stir-fry the leeks for a few minutes until tender. Remove from the heat and quickly stir in the cheese and half the toasted pumpkin and sunflower seeds.

Divide the mixture equally between the pancakes and roll them up. Arrange them in a hot buttered ovenproof dish, cover with foil and reheat briefly in a moderate oven. Sprinkle with the remaining toasted seeds and parsley and serve immediately with a green salad. (Serves 6)

*G*OATS' CHEESE IN PUFF PASTRY PARCELS

Any strong-flavoured cheese can be used in this recipe, which is particularly good served with the damson chutney so popular in Lakeland.

300 g (10 oz) puff pastry
175 g (6 oz) goats' cheese
A little milk, to glaze

Pre-heat the oven to 200°C (400°F, gas mark 6).

Roll out the pastry thinly on a lightly floured surface. Cut into 6 squares. Cut the cheese into 6 slices and place a circle of cheese in the centre of each square of pastry. Dampen the edges of the pastry with a little milk and fold around the cheese.

Place on a baking tray, seam side down, and make a small hole in the top of each parcel to let out the steam during cooking. Brush with milk and bake in a hot oven for about 20 minutes, or until golden brown and crisp.

Serve hot with spiced chutney (see page 165) and a green salad, or leave until cold for a picnic. (Serves 6)

CARROT, PARSNIP AND CHEESE ROAST

Beatrix and Willie received food parcels during the Second World War from Beatrix's many American friends and admirers. In a letter to Bertha Mahoney Miller dated 18 June, 1942, Beatrix thanks her for the latest parcel. 'Your charming present arrived unexpectedly this morning – Lemon Juice! Also butter, dextrose, onion flakes, chocolate, bacon and cheese.' Beatrix considered the rationing 'very just; a bit inconvenient for country people far removed from shops', though she was having to do more cooking than usual. 'It does make some work, as the only chance is to do all the cooking oneself, including the hens' and the sheep dogs'!'

Root vegetables like carrots and parsnips were used as sweeteners in the war. Any combination can be used in this savoury recipe and the bacon may be omitted. For a change, try substituting rolled oats for half the breadcrumbs.

900 g (2 lb) carrots, roughly chopped
700 g (1½ lb) parsnips, roughly chopped
4–6 tablespoons (⅓ – ½ cup) fromage frais
½ teaspoon freshly grated nutmeg
Salt and freshly milled black pepper
50 g (2 oz/¼ cup) butter
1 large onion, finely chopped
2 large cloves of garlic, crushed
250 g (8 oz) smoked streaky bacon rashers
175 g (6 oz/2 cups) fresh wholemeal breadcrumbs
175 g (6 oz/1½ cups) grated Cheddar or Lancashire cheese
1 tablespoon dried marjoram

Steam or boil the carrots and parsnips together until very tender, then reduce them to a purée in a blender or food processor with the fromage frais. Season well with the nutmeg, salt and plenty of black pepper.

Pre-heat the oven to 230°C (450°F, gas mark 8).

Melt the butter in a frying pan and fry the onion and garlic until soft and transparent. Stir into the vegetable purée, then turn the mixture into a buttered, shallow ovenproof dish. Chop the bacon into pieces and fry over a high heat until crisp. Using a slotted spoon, spread on the top of the root purée in an even layer. Reserve the bacon fat.

Put the breadcrumbs into a bowl and stir in the grated cheese and marjoram. Sprinkle evenly over the bacon, then dribble the reserved bacon fat over the top. Bake on the top shelf of a hot oven for about 30 minutes, or until the topping is a bubbling golden crust. Serve hot with a crisp green salad. (Serves 6)

From The Story of A Fierce Bad Rabbit

*C*HEESY LEEK AND SWEET-POTATO CAKES

At the end of Beatrix Potter's story The Tale of Little Pig Robinson, *Robinson eventually escapes from the 'Pound of Candles' sailing ship, where he is being fattened up by the cook to serve with apple sauce, and lands on the island of the Bong tree. 'The shore was covered with oysters. Acid drops and sweets grew upon the trees. Yams, which are a sort of sweet potato, abounded ready cooked. The bread-fruit tree grew iced cakes and muffins, ready baked; so no pig need sigh for porridge.' Robinson lived happily ever after on the island, getting 'fatter and fatter and more fatterer'. So don't eat* too *many of these delicious potato cakes! Any variety of potatoes, or yams themselves, may be used in this recipe.*

900 g (2 lb) sweet potatoes
125 g (4 oz/½ cup) butter
2 (3 US) tablespoons thick natural yoghurt
2 (3 US) level tablespoons wholegrain mustard
2 teaspoons dried thyme
Salt and freshly milled black pepper
2 medium leeks, finely sliced
Fine wholemeal breadcrumbs
Grated cheese
Sunflower oil for frying
Toasted sesame seeds for sprinkling (optional)

Peel the sweet potatoes, cut them up roughly and steam or boil them until tender. Drain well and mash. Turn into a mixing bowl and stir in half the butter, the yoghurt, mustard and thyme. Season well with salt and pepper.

Melt the remaining butter in a saucepan, add the leeks and cook over a gentle heat until just soft, stirring frequently. Mix this buttery leek mixture into the potato purée and leave until cold. Using wet hands, shape handfuls of the mixture into flat cakes. Mix equal quantities of breadcrumbs and cheese and coat the sweet potato cakes with this mixture.

Fry in hot sunflower oil over a moderate heat until golden brown on both sides. Sprinkle with toasted sesame seeds if you wish and drain well on kitchen paper. Serve sizzling hot with a mixed salad, accompanied with bacon if you wish, or spread with cream cheese or herb and garlic cheese.

From The Tale of Little Pig Robinson

Vegetables and Salads

POTATO AND CELERIAC PURÉE

When the Potter family first rented Heath Park, in Scotland, for their summer holiday, they discovered the house was in some disrepair, as the owners had been away in India for many years. The house stood in one acre of ground, but Beatrix's journal records, 'About half the ground is stocked with "40-fold" potatoes, which through want of "manure", to quote McDougall [their gamekeeper], are only the size of walnuts, but sweet.' A really well-made vegetable purée is delicious. The secret is to dry the vegetables out sufficiently before adding butter and cream.

450 g (l lb) celeriac, when prepared
Juice of ½ lemon
450 g (1 lb) floury potatoes, when prepared
50 g (2 oz/¼ cup) unsalted butter
4 (5 US) tablespoons double or clotted cream
Salt and freshly milled black pepper
Freshly grated nutmeg
Chopped fresh parsley or chervil

Wash, trim and peel the celeriac, then weigh it. Cut into even-sized chunks and put immediately into water with the lemon juice added to prevent discoloration. Cook in lightly salted chicken or vegetable stock or water for about 20 minutes or until quite tender. Peel the potatoes, weigh them, then cook in lightly salted water until tender. Drain both vegetables, then return them to their pans to dry out the excess moisture over a low heat.

Pass the vegetables through a sieve or food-mill directly into a basin lined with muslin. Allow the purée to cool and drain well, twisting the muslin to help this process. (It is important to remove all the excess liquid or the purée will be watery.)

Melt the butter and cream in a non-stick pan and season well with pepper and nutmeg. Lower the heat and add the cool purée, a spoonful at a time, stirring well all the time with a wooden spoon. You will probably need to add more cream as you go along – this depends on the amount of liquid extracted from the vegetables. When the purée is steaming hot, taste and adjust seasoning, then pile into a warmed serving dish and sprinkle with parsley or chervil. Serve with roast duck, goose, lamb or game. (Serves 6)

Variations

The dish is also good covered with grated Parmesan cheese and browned lightly under the grill.

Many other root vegetables make marvellous purées, either on their own or in combination. Here are a few suggestions: salsify and parsnip; scorzonera and potato; turnip and potato; parsnip and carrot; parsnip, carrot and celeriac; Jerusalem artichoke and potato.

POTATO PANCAKE STUFFED WITH WILD MUSHROOMS

Beatrix Potter grew potatoes at Hill Top and Castle Cottage, and both she and her husband Willie were very fond of them. 'There are probably more disputes over bacon and plain potatoes than any other eatable,' Beatrix observed in the early months of their marriage.

For the pancake

125 g (4 oz) freshly cooked floury potatoes
2 eggs, separated
Salt and freshly milled black pepper
25 g (1 oz/2 US tablespoons) butter

For the filling

25 g (1 oz/2 US tablespoons) butter
½ a small onion, finely chopped
½ a clove garlic, crushed
125 g (4 oz/1½ cups) sliced assorted wild mushrooms
1 tablespoon chopped fresh parsley or chervil
Salt and freshly milled black pepper
Freshly grated nutmeg
1 tablespoon double cream or crème fraîche
(optional)

This delicious recipe makes a pancake for one person; simply increase the quantities as required.

Sieve the cooked potato into a bowl, then beat in the egg yolks. Season with salt and pepper. Whisk the egg whites until stiff, then fold into the potato mixture.

To make the filling, heat the butter in a small pan and gently fry the onion and garlic until soft. Turn up the heat and stir in the mushrooms. Cook for about 5 minutes, then stir in the parsley or chervil. Season with salt, pepper and nutmeg, then stir in the cream, if using. Keep warm while you make the pancake.

Heat the butter in a 15-cm (6-in) heavy frying pan and tip in the potato mixture. Cook until golden on the under side, then turn over and cook the other side. Spoon on the mushroom mixture, then fold over and serve immediately. (Serves 1)

STUFFED PARASOL MUSHROOMS

In a picture letter to Winifred Warne dated 6 September, 1905, Beatrix Potter describes picking 'such lots of mushrooms' in the fields at Gwaynynog, in Wales, the home of her uncle Fred Burton.

From the size of some of the mushrooms, they could have been parasols, which can grow very large – up to 25 cm (10 in) in diameter. They are one of the tastiest of our edible fungi and grow in grassy meadows, orchards, woodland clearings or by roadsides from July to November. If you are lucky, you may even find a parasol growing on the back lawn.

Parasols are best picked just as the cap has flattened, but before it begins to turn up slightly at the edges; twist or cut them from the ground. They can be stored for up to 24 hours in a cool, dry place. After this, they begin to take on a rusty tinge and the flavour becomes stronger.

Because of their shape, parasol mushrooms are ideal for stuffing, but any large flat mushrooms may be used in this recipe. (NB Seek expert help if you are uncertain about identifying any edible mushrooms.)

6 medium parasols or 12 large flat mushrooms
4 sticks of celery, finely chopped
1 small onion, finely chopped
2 cloves of garlic, crushed
50 g (2 oz/½ cup) hazelnuts or walnuts, finely chopped
75 g (3 oz/6 US tablespoons) butter
75 g (3 oz/1 cup) fresh wholemeal breadcrumbs
2 (3 US) tablespoons chopped fresh parsley
2 teaspoons lemon juice
Salt and freshly milled black pepper
1 large egg, beaten
50 g (2 oz/½ cup) grated Cheddar or Lancashire cheese
2 (3 US) tablespoons chicken stock

Pre-heat the oven to 180°C (350°F, gas mark 4).

Wipe the mushrooms, but don't peel them. Check around the top of the stems for insects, then remove and discard the stems. (If using another type of mushroom, remove the stalks, chop finely and add them to the stuffing.) Mix the celery, onion, garlic and nuts (and mushroom stalks, if using) together in a bowl. Heat the butter in a large frying pan and lightly fry the skin side of the mushrooms, a few at a time. Remove from the pan and reserve.

Fry the celery mixture quickly for 2–3 minutes, stirring occasionally. Remove from the heat and stir in the breadcrumbs, parsley and lemon juice and season to taste. Bind together with the egg. Spoon into the mushroom caps and place them side by side in a shallow ovenproof dish just large enough to hold them. Sprinkle a little cheese over each mushroom and pour the stock around the edges of the dish. Bake in a moderate oven for 20–25 minutes.

Serve hot with a crisp green salad. (Serves 6)

Above: Marrow in a tomato and ginger sauce

ℳARROW IN A TOMATO AND GINGER SAUCE

In The Tale of The Flopsy Bunnies, *Benjamin and his wife Flopsy managed to rescue their offspring from the sack in which they had been imprisoned by Mr McGregor. To take their place, Benjamin and Flopsy stuffed the sack with three rotten vegetable marrows, an old blacking-brush and two decayed turnips. One of the rotten marrows later came flying through the kitchen window and hit the youngest Flopsy Bunny when the McGregors discovered they had been cheated of fat young rabbits.*
A fresh marrow would be best for this recipe!

1 tablespoon olive oil
l large onion, chopped
2 large cloves of garlic, crushed
1 medium marrow or 4–6 zucchini (courgettes)
700 g (1½ lb) tomatoes
2.5 cm (1 in) knob of fresh ginger root, shredded finely
2 (3 US) tablespoons tomato purée
½ teaspoon caster sugar
2 bay leaves
1 tablespoon chopped fresh parsley
1 tablespoon chopped fresh basil or 1 teaspoon dried
Pinch of dried thyme
Salt and freshly milled black pepper

98

Heat the oil in a pan and gently fry the onion and garlic for about 5 minutes, until soft. Peel, seed and chop the marrow into cubes. Add to the onion and cook for a further 5 minutes. Skin and roughly chop the tomatoes and add to the pan with all the other ingredients. Cover the pan and simmer gently for about 30 minutes, or until the vegetables are tender.

Taste and adjust the seasoning as necessary. Bubble over a high heat to reduce a little if watery (depending on the juiciness of the tomatoes). Serve immediately with grilled or roast meat, fish and poultry, or serve chilled as a starter or light main dish. This recipe can be made using mixed root vegetables instead of marrow. (Serves 6)

SWEET-AND-SOUR RED CABBAGE

*Beatrix Potter grew both red and green cabbage
in the vegetable garden at Hill Top. She wrote to
Millie Warne in August, 1912, in the middle of what was
obviously a bad summer in the Lake District, 'It is a
grand season for cabbages! The caterpillars
are all drowned.' She was certainly a gardener
with a sense of humour.
This red cabbage dish will freeze and reheat very
successfully, so it can be made in advance. (In fact I think
the flavour improves with reheating.)*

900 g (2 lb) firm red cabbage
450 g (1 lb) cooking or firm eating apples
450 g (1 lb) onions, when prepared
Salt and freshly milled black pepper
¼ whole nutmeg, freshly grated
½ teaspoon ground cloves
½ teaspoon ground cinnamon
1 large clove of garlic, crushed
1 tablespoon red wine vinegar
Brown sugar, to taste
A small knob of butter

Pre-heat the oven to 170°C (325°F, gas mark 3).

Discard the tough outer leaves of the cabbage, cut into quarters and remove the hard stalk. Shred the remaining cabbage finely. Peel, core and roughly chop the apples. Peel and finely slice the onions (then weigh them).

Mix all the vegetables in a large bowl and season with salt, pepper, nutmeg, cloves, cinnamon and garlic. Mix again thoroughly, then transfer into a suitable lidded casserole dish. Pour over the vinegar and add 1 dessertspoon brown sugar, to start with, and the butter. Cover with a lid and cook in a fairly low oven for 2–2½ hours, or until tender, but not mushy. Stir once or twice during the cooking; taste and add more sugar if necessary.

Serve with pork and lamb dishes, tatie pot (see page 44), sausages, duck, goose and game. This vegetable dish will keep warm for quite a while without coming to any harm. (Serves 6)

TIMMY TIPTOES' FAVOURITE NUT BURGERS

The Tale of Timmy Tiptoes was written to please Beatrix Potter's many American readers, and was a new venture for her in terms of the animals she portrayed. Instead of the familiar rabbits, mice, ducks, foxes and badgers, a pair of chipmunks and a large black bear roam the Sawrey woods. Timmy Tiptoes is chased by the other grey squirrels into the trunk of a hollow tree. Plied with nuts by Mr Chippy Hackee, who is living there, Timmy becomes so fat that he has to wait until the tree is blown down before he can be reunited with his wife, Goody.
Don't let that put you off eating these nutritious and tasty burgers.

75 g (3 oz/½ cup) ground roasted nuts (hazelnuts, peanuts, cashews or almonds)
1 large onion, finely chopped
1 small green pepper, seeded and finely chopped
2 sticks of celery, finely chopped
1 large clove of garlic, crushed (optional)
3 tablespoons (¼ cup) finely chopped cabbage
3 tablespoons (¼ cup) fresh wholemeal breadcrumbs
1 tablespoon chopped fresh mixed herbs
3 tablespoons (¼ cup) wheatgerm
Large pinch of cayenne pepper
Large pinch of ground mace
1 large egg
1½ (2 US) tablespoons tomato purée
1½ (2 US) tablespoons natural yoghurt
Salt and freshly milled black pepper
Beaten egg, for coating
About 175 g (6 oz/1½ cups) dry wholemeal breadcrumbs

Mix the nuts with the onion, green pepper, celery, garlic (if using), cabbage, fresh breadcrumbs, herbs and wheatgerm in a large mixing bowl. Stir in the cayenne and mace. Place the egg, tomato purée and yoghurt in a small bowl and whisk together. Stir into the nut mixture and season to taste with salt and pepper.

Form the mixture into 12 small burgers, adding a little more yoghurt if necessary. Cover and chill for a few hours in the fridge to firm them up and prevent them breaking up during cooking.

Pre-heat the oven to 180°C (350°F, gas mark 4).

Dip each burger into the beaten egg first, then into the dry breadcrumbs, and place on a well-greased baking tray. Bake for 15 minutes, then turn the burgers over with a fish-slice and bake for a further 15 minutes. Serve in a wholemeal bun with home-made tomato sauce or natural yoghurt and a crisp green salad. (Serves 6)

*Y*ARBY PUDDEN

Country cooks in years gone by would often use the first green leaves of spring in dumplings and suet puddings. The traditional Lakeland dish was yarby pudden, or easter-ledge pudding, which was served at Easter with lamb. It was made from bistort, or easter-ledge, a plant with pale pink brush-like flowers which grows wild round the shores of Esthwaite, amongst other places in Lakeland. The other essential ingredient in the traditional herb pudding was lady's mantle, which was held to derive magical powers from the glittering beads of dew the blossoms collect. Both plants are easily grown in your garden, but many alternative mixtures of plants can be used: very young nettles, young dandelions, chives, spinach, sorrel, spring cabbage, sprout tops, curly kale, or raspberry, blackcurrant or gooseberry leaves.

Many people in Lakeland still talk about this savoury pudding, but few seem to make it now, although it tastes excellent and 'keeps your complexions good'. Beatrix Potter would have eaten it regularly as a spring tonic; the herb pudding offered by Timmy Willie to Johnny Town-mouse in The Tale of Johnny Town-Mouse *must have been the cleansing easter-ledge pudding. Mollie Green from Anvil Cottage remembers being sent out of school with fellow pupils to collect easter-ledges; probably for the teacher's supper as they were also eaten as a vegetable.*

450 g (1 lb) young easter-ledges, picked when they are about 10 cm (4 in) high
1 medium onion or leek, finely chopped
250 g (8 oz) pearl barley
Salt and freshly milled black pepper
50 g (2 oz/¼ cup) butter
3 eggs, lightly beaten

Wash the pearl barley well in cold water, then drain. Strip the easter-ledge leaves from the stalks and wash well. Dry in a cloth, then chop coarsely, discarding the stalks. (Treat any other greenstuff in the same way.)

Mix the chopped leaves with the onion or leek and drained barley. Season well with salt and pepper, then turn the mixture into a colander lined with muslin. Tie it up loosely so that it forms a round shape, then lower into a pan of boiling water. Poach very gently for 1½ hours.

Lift the pudding out and drain in a colander for a few seconds. Melt the butter in a saucepan, then untie the pudding and turn the contents into the saucepan. Heat through gently, stirring well with a wooden spoon. Just before serving, season the lightly beaten eggs and stir into the pudding. Continue stirring until the eggs scramble.

Serve immediately as a vegetable with lamb, sausages, game, bacon or veal. It also makes an excellent vegetarian dish on its own. (Serves 6)

Variation

In some parts of Cumbria, people beat just 1 egg into the barley mixture, then make it into a cake and fry it in fat to eat with bacon and eggs, or fried potatoes.

CUCUMBER AND STRAWBERRY SALAD

*When Beatrix Potter first bought Hill Top,
her farm in the Lakeland village of Near Sawrey,
she discovered the house was overrun with rats. She
wrote to Millie Warne, of the publishing family, about
her battle with them, 'The rats have come
back in great force, two big ones were trapped
in the shed here, beside turning out a nest of 8 baby
rats in the cucumber frame opposite the door.' The Tale
of Samuel Whiskers was based upon the imaginary
adventures of a pair of Hill Top rats.
Cucumber combines very well with strawberries,
both of which Beatrix grew at Hill Top, giving a lovely
fresh-tasting salad which goes particularly nicely with cold
salmon or sea trout. For a special occasion, splash
over a little champagne instead of wine!*

1 large cucumber (2 American cucumbers)
250–350 g (8–12 oz) large strawberries
Salt and freshly milled black pepper
Pinch of caster sugar
3 tablespoons (¼ cup) dry white wine
1 tablespoon chopped fresh tarragon
A few borage flowers, to decorate

Remove the peel, if you wish, before thinly slicing the cucumber, otherwise wipe the cucumber, leave the peel on and slice. Hull and thickly slice the strawberries.

Arrange alternate circles of cucumber and straw-berries in a shallow serving dish. Season with salt, plenty of black pepper and caster sugar. Spoon over the dry white wine and sprinkle with tarragon. Chill well.

Decorate with a few blue borage flowers and serve with cold salmon, sea trout or chicken. (Serves 6)

WATERCRESS, ENDIVE, ORANGE AND BRAZIL-NUT SALAD

1 head curly endive, or frisée
1 bunch watercress or corn salad
3 large oranges
1 medium onion, peeled
75 g (3 oz) Brazil or macadamia nuts

For the dressing

Grated rind and juice of 1 large orange
150 ml (¼ pint/⅔ cup) natural yoghurt
1 tablespoon chopped fresh mint (optional)
Salt and freshly milled black pepper

Wash and dry the endive and tear into pieces. Wash and trim the watercress or corn salad, tearing it into small sprigs. Remove all the peel and pith from the oranges and slice across into thin rounds. Cut the onion into very fine rings, separate them and put into a sieve. Dip them into a pan of boiling water for 15 seconds only, then refresh under cold running water and pat dry. (This removes some of the strong flavour. You can, of course, use the onion raw if you prefer.) Thickly slice the nuts.

Arrange the endive and watercress in a salad bowl or on 6 individual plates. Garnish with slices of orange and top with the onion rings.

To make the dressing, put the grated orange rind and juice into a small bowl. Whisk in the yoghurt and stir in the mint, if using. Season to taste with salt and pepper, then chill well. Just before serving, drizzle the dressing over the salad and sprinkle with the nuts.

The salad is excellent with goose, duck, feathered game, pork and ham. (Serves 6)

*Cucumber and strawberry salad, decorated with violets in spring, and
served alongside watercress, endive, orange and Brazil-nut salad*

RED-CHERRY AND CLOVER SUMMER SALAD

*In 1894 Beatrix wrote in her journal, 'I have been tying
up some bunches [of cherries] in little muslin bags,
also weeding, to the amusement of the old gardener.'
Use a mixture of red and green salad leaves
for this colourful salad, such as Red Salad Bowl,
Lollo Rosso, Cos, Webbs, and oak-leaf lettuce; whatever
variety, it must be crisp.*

Salad leaves of various types, as available
2 bunches of radishes
¼ cucumber (½ American cucumber), sliced
250 g (8 oz) red cherries
50 g (2 oz/⅓ cup) pine nuts

For the dressing

Large pinch of coarse sea salt
1 clove of garlic
1 tablespoon fruit vinegar (eg, raspberry vinegar,
page 146) or white wine vinegar
Freshly milled black pepper
6 tablespoons (½ cup) olive oil
30 red clover flowers

Wash and dry the salad leaves and wash and trim the
radishes. Soak the radishes in ice-cold water, to make
them really crisp, while you prepare the dressing.
Grind the salt in a pestle and mortar, then add the
garlic. Crush with the salt. Stir in the vinegar and
plenty of black pepper, then beat in the oil. Lastly,
mix in the clover flowers and leave for 30 minutes for
the flowers to infuse.

Tear the salad leaves into small pieces and arrange
in a large salad bowl, or 6 individual bowls or plates.
Slice the radishes and cut the cucumber slices in half,
then add to the salad. Stone the cherries and arrange
on top. Sprinkle with the pine nuts, then spoon the
clover dressing over the salad. Serve immediately.
(Serves 6)

THE GOOD RABBIT'S SALAD OF CARROTS, COURGETTES AND NASTURTIUM FLOWERS

Beatrix Potter wrote The Story of A Fierce
Bad Rabbit *for Louie Warne, the daughter of
her publisher, Harold. Louie had thought Peter Rabbit
was far too good and demanded a tale about
a really naughty rabbit. The story is very simple:
the fierce bad Rabbit steals the good Rabbit's carrot,
but justice arrives in the shape of a man with a gun, who
'sees something sitting on a bench. He thinks
it is a very funny bird!' He shoots and all that remains
on the bench is a carrot, tail and whiskers. Beatrix was
dissatisfied with her picture of the hunter holding his gun
and sent a replacement to Warne's after her
marriage to Willie, who knew about these things,
but it was never used.
This lovely summery salad includes nasturtium
leaves and flowers, which Beatrix grew in her garden at
Hill Top. She also grew carrots in the vegetable garden.*

3–4 medium young carrots
3–4 medium courgettes
12 young nasturtium leaves
50 g (2 oz/⅓ cup) pumpkin seeds
50 g (2 oz/⅓ cup) sunflower seeds
50 g (2 oz/⅓ cup) flaked almonds
12 orange nasturtium flowers
Chopped fresh basil, to garnish

For the dressing

1 teaspoon coarse sea salt
½ clove of garlic
1 teaspoon basil vinegar (see page 168, herb
vinegars) or white wine vinegar
Freshly milled black pepper
1 teaspoon mild wholegrain mustard
2 (3 US) tablespoons walnut oil
4 tablespoons (⅓ cup) olive oil
Orange juice, to taste

Scrub and coarsely grate the carrots and courgettes. Wash and slice the nasturtium leaves. Dry fry the pumpkin seeds, sunflower seeds and flaked almonds in a frying pan over a high heat until toasted, but not burnt. Wash and dry the nasturtium flowers, remove the stems and tear into petals.

To make the dressing, crush the salt in a pestle and mortar, then add the garlic. Pound it with the salt, then add the vinegar, plenty of freshly milled black pepper and the mustard. Finally add the oils. Pour everything into a screw-top jar and shake vigorously until thoroughly blended. Taste and adjust seasoning as necessary, adding orange juice to taste.

Just before serving, toss the prepared carrots, courgettes and nasturtium leaves in the dressing with the seeds. Divide between 6 individual salad bowls or plates and decorate with nasturtium petals. Sprinkle over chopped basil. (Serves 6)

*C*OUNTRYWOMAN'S HERB GARDEN SALAD

You can really use your imagination with this country salad; the important thing is that you keep to shades of green, apart from the decorative flowers. Pick all the greenstuff in the spring, when leaves are young and tender. This is just the type of salad which would have been made by a countrywoman like Beatrix Potter. Most of the ingredients would have been grown in her gardens at Hill Top and Castle Cottage.
Make the base of the salad with lettuce, lamb's lettuce and spinach and include only small quantities of sorrel, rocket, dandelion and purslane, as they tend to be rather sharp-flavoured. A few leaves of each herb will probably be enough. To ring the changes and for later in the year, when many of the wild plants have grown bitter and coarse, introduce different varieties of lettuce, cucumber, peas, avocado, broad beans, mange-tout, broccoli florets, celery, shredded Brussels sprouts, apple, cabbage, leeks, and so on. The dressing is very thick and superb.

Lettuce thinnings
Lamb's lettuce or watercress
Young spinach leaves
Young sorrel leaves
Salad rocket
Young dandelion leaves and a few flowers
Young purslane sprigs
6 spring onions
Fresh chives and chive flowers
Sprigs of salad burnet
Fresh applemint or peppermint leaves
Fresh tarragon leaves
Sprigs of fresh fennel
Angelica leaves
Lovage leaves

For the dressing

150 ml (¼ pint/⅔ cup) sunflower oil
1 teaspoon herb, flower or fruit vinegar (see pages 146, 168 and 170)
1 (1½ US) tablespoon mild French mustard
1 small clove of garlic, crushed
Freshly milled black pepper
2 (3 US) tablespoons chopped fresh parsley or chervil

Collect a selection of salad leaves together, depending on what you have available. Wash all the greens thoroughly and dry well. Tear the larger leaves into small pieces with your fingers and shred the sharp saladstuffs like sorrel, rocket, angelica and lovage quite finely with scissors. Place all the greens in a large salad bowl or 6 individual bowls or plates. Chop the spring onions and chives finely and add to the salad. Scatter the herb leaves on top and decorate with a few chive and dandelion flowers.

To make the dressing, put the oil into a small bowl. Add the vinegar and the mustard. Using a balloon whisk, beat the mixture together to make a thick emulsion. Add the garlic and plenty of black pepper. Whisk together again, then add the parsley or chervil. Taste and adjust seasoning as necessary.

Serve the salad with the dressing in a small bowl so that everyone can help themselves. (Serves 6)

Puddings

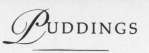

Spotted Rum Dog 108

Blackberry and Apple Upside-down Cake 108

Treacle and Ginger Pudding 109

Witherslack Damson Cobbler 110

Warm Sticky Gingerbread with Cumberland Rum Butter 111

Dorset Apple and Lemon Tart 112

Westmorland Walnut and Raisin Tart 112

Cumberland Rum Nicky 113

Damson Fool in Brandy-Snap Baskets 114

Sawrey Rhubarb and Apricot Pie 116

Blackcurrant and Meadowsweet Snow 117

Tullythwaite Apricot Creams 118

Elderflower Fritters with Gooseberry Purée 120

Redcurrant and Raspberry Ice-Cream 120

Flopsy Bunnies' Ice-Cream Surprise 121

Wild Strawberry Syllabub 121

SPOTTED RUM DOG

The Roly-Poly Pudding, *later to be called* The Tale of Samuel Whiskers, *was very much a celebration of Hill Top, the Lakeland farm which Beatrix Potter had bought in 1905. The book is set inside the farmhouse, much of which has remained unchanged to this day.*
The Roly-Poly Pudding *featured, and was dedicated to, her pet white rat, Samuel Whiskers, who with his wife, Anna Maria, captured poor Tom Kitten and made him into a 'kitten dumpling roly-poly pudding'. Luckily, he was rescued by the little dog carpenter John Joiner, and the dumpling was peeled off him and 'made into a bag pudding, with currants in it to hide the smuts'.*
Perhaps this pudding should be called spotted rum kitten!

175 g (6 oz/scant 1 cup) dried fruit – a mixture of currants, raisins and sultanas
3 tablespoons (¼ cup) dark rum
250 g (8 oz/1⅔ cups) self-raising flour
Pinch of salt
1 teaspoon mixed spice
125 g (4 oz) shredded suet
75 g (3 oz/6 tablespoons) caster or soft brown sugar
Finely grated rind of 1 lemon
About 120 ml (4 fl oz/½ cup) milk

Soak the fruit in the rum for at least 1 hour, until plump. Sieve the flour with the salt and spice into a mixing bowl. Stir in the suet, sugar, lemon rind and soaked dry fruit, including any liquor. Using a palette knife, stir in enough milk to give a soft, elastic dough. Knead very lightly until smooth, then shape into a neat roll about 20 cm (8 in) long.

Butter a large piece of foil and place the pudding on it. Wrap up loosely into a parcel, allowing room for expansion during cooking. Steam over boiling water in a large steamer, a fish kettle or on a rack in a roasting tin for an hour, until well-risen and firm.

Unwrap and serve hot, cut into thick slices, with a generous dollop of rum butter (see page 111) on each portion, or with homemade custard or thick cream. (Serves 6)

Variation

BAKED RUM DOG

Make as before, then place the pudding on a piece of buttered foil or greaseproof paper large enough to come halfway up the sides of the roll. Fold up the foil or paper at the ends, then place on a greased baking tray. Brush with a mixture of beaten egg and milk, then bake in the centre of a fairly hot oven (200°C, 400°F, gas mark 6) for about 40 minutes, or until well-risen and golden brown.

Remove from the oven and sprinkle with caster sugar. Serve with rum butter, custard or thick cream.

BLACKBERRY AND APPLE UPSIDE-DOWN CAKE

Beatrix Potter wrote to her friend Millie Warne soon after she bought Hill Top Farm, telling her that she was absorbed in gardening. 'The apples on the old trees prove to be very good cookers, we have had some for dinner.'
I am sure she would have enjoyed this old-fashioned apple pudding.

25 g (1 oz/2 US tablespoons) butter
2 (3 US) level tablespoons clear honey
2 large Cox's or other firm eating apples
250 g (8 oz/1 pint) blackberries
125 g (4 oz/½ cup) butter or margarine
125 g (4 oz/½ cup) caster or soft brown sugar
2 large eggs, beaten
125 g (4 oz/¾ cup) white or wholemeal self-raising flour
2 teaspoons ground cinnamon
About 1 tablespoon cold water

Pre-heat the oven to 180°C (350°F, gas mark 4).
Mix the 1 oz (2 tablespoons) of butter with the honey and spread over the base of a 20-cm (8-in) round cake tin which is at least 5-cm (2-in) deep. Peel and core the apples and chop into roughly 12-mm

(½-in) cubes. Arrange them with the blackberries over the honey and butter in the cake tin.

Cream the remaining quantity of fat with the sugar until light and fluffy, then beat in the eggs, a little at a time. Sieve the flour with the cinnamon and fold very gently into the creamed mixture. Stir in sufficient water to make a soft dropping consistency, then cover the fruit evenly with the cake mixture. Bake near the top of a moderate oven for about 30 minutes, or until well-risen and golden brown.

Remove from the oven and leave to cool in the tin for a few minutes, then turn out on to a warm serving plate. Leave the tin on top of the plate for 2–3 minutes for all the juices to run into the sponge, then remove. Serve warm with soured cream or yoghurt. (Serves 6)

Variations

Several different fruit combinations can be used for this versatile pudding: raspberry and apple, raspberry and pear, blackberry and pear, rhubarb and apple, and many more.

*T*REACLE AND GINGER PUDDING

Beatrix Potter writes in her journal from her uncle and aunt's home in North Wales, 'We had a picnic tea . . . provided by Polly . . . She made a most excellent treacle-pudding which, combined with the thunder, had disastrous effects upon Alice and me, and finally Polly herself.' Perhaps Beatrix should have heeded the advice given by old Mr Paget, an eccentric friend of the Potter family in London, 'The only use for a rich pudding is to put your foot in it.' How I disagree with him, as she obviously did! I think the 'excellent treacle-pudding' must have been a treacle tart, as the occasion was a picnic, but this pudding is also 'most excellent'.

125 g (4 oz/¾ cup) white or wholemeal self-raising flour
Pinch of salt
2 heaped teaspoons ground ginger
125 g (4 oz/1⅓ cups) fresh white or brown breadcrumbs
125 g (4 oz) shredded suet
2 (3 US) heaped tablespoons golden syrup
About 3 tablespoons (¼ cup) milk
25 g (1 oz/¼ cup) chopped stem ginger

Sieve the flour, salt and ginger together into a mixing bowl. Stir in the breadcrumbs and suet. Melt the syrup over a gentle heat until just runny, then add the milk. Pour into the dry ingredients and mix together well. Lastly, add the chopped ginger and mix again, adding a little extra milk if necessary to make a soft dropping consistency.

Turn the mixture into a greased 900-ml (1½-pint/1-quart US) pudding basin. Cover with pleated buttered greaseproof paper and foil (allowing room for expansion) and steam for 2–2½ hours, or until firm and well-risen. Serve hot with homemade custard, or more warm syrup and thick cream. (Serves 6)

Variation

*S*POTTED TREACLE AND GINGER PUDDING

Add 125 g (4 oz/⅔ cup) currants with the breadcrumbs and suet, then continue as before.

A Witherslack damson cobbler from the Cedar Manor Hotel, Windermere

WITHERSLACK DAMSON COBBLER

Cumbria's best-known fruit is the damson and the finest damsons of all grow in a fertile area running south of Windermere, known as the Lyth Valley. Locally they are known as Witherslack damsons, after the village of that name. This version of damson cobbler is based on a recipe given to me by Lynn Hadley, from the Cedar Manor Hotel in Windermere.

900 g (2 lb) damsons
3 tablespoons (¼ cup) cold water
Sugar, to taste
250 g (8 oz/1⅔ cups) self-raising flour
1 teaspoon baking powder
50 g (2 oz/¼ cup) caster sugar
50 g (2 oz/¼ cup) butter or margarine
1 egg mixed with enough milk to make 150 ml
(¼ pint/⅔ cup)
Extra milk, to glaze

Pre-heat the oven to 190°C (375°F, gas mark 5).

Wash the damsons and remove any stalks. Place in a large saucepan with the water, cover and simmer gently for about 15 minutes, or until tender. Remove as many stones as possible and add sugar to taste. Pour into a greased ovenproof dish deep enough to be only about half full.

To make the scone topping, sieve the flour with the baking powder into a large mixing bowl. Stir in the sugar and rub in the fat. Mix to a soft dough with the egg and milk mixture, then knead very lightly.

Roll or pat out on a lightly floured surface to a thickness of about 12 mm (½ in), then cut out into 12 rounds using a 5-cm (2-in) cutter. Place the pastry circles over the damsons in an overlapping ring around the dish. Brush with milk and bake in a fairly hot oven for about 30 minutes, or until well-risen and golden brown. Serve warm with pouring cream, *crème fraîche*, yoghurt, or homemade custard.

Many other fruits may be used instead of damsons. (Serves 6)

WARM STICKY GINGERBREAD WITH CUMBERLAND RUM BUTTER

Gingerbread has always been popular in Lakeland. In Beatrix Potter's day, it was made from oatmeal, and was more like parkin than the spongy version we know today. Eleanor Quinlan and her husband Richard (pictured below), who run the Mill, a well-known hotel in Mungrisdale near Penrith, gave me this recipe for a sticky gingerbread. She serves it with Cumberland rum butter in the traditional way. According to legend, rum butter was first discovered by a little old lady, whose dubiously acquired cask of rum leaked over her brown sugar and butter stores. She had never tasted 'owt better', so from that day she continued to make rum butter. In Cumbria, rum butter and oatcakes used to be given to friends who called to see a new baby. In return they would leave a silver coin. Plenty of coins in the empty butter bowl meant that the child would never be wanting.

For the gingerbread

250 g (8 oz/1 cup) black treacle
250 g (8 oz/1 cup) demerara sugar
250 g (8 oz/1 cup) butter
2 large eggs, beaten
350 g (12 oz/2½ cups) strong plain flour
Pinch of salt
2 level dessertspoons (1½ US tablespoons) ground ginger
2 level dessertspoons (1½ US tablespoons) ground cinnamon
A little freshly grated nutmeg
300 ml (½ pint/1¼ cups) warm milk
2 level teaspoons bicarbonate of soda

For the rum butter

250 g (8 oz/1 cup) soft brown sugar
¼ nutmeg, freshly grated
2–3 tablespoons (¼ cup) dark rum
125 g (4 oz/½ cup) unsalted butter

Pre-heat the oven to 150°C (300°F, gas mark 2).

Put the treacle, sugar and butter in a saucepan and melt over a gentle heat, stirring all the time. Remove from the heat and stir in the beaten eggs. Sieve the flour with the salt and spices into a large mixing bowl and stir in the melted treacle mixture. In a separate bowl, pour the warm milk over the bicarbonate of soda and stir well. Add to the flour and treacle mixture and mix together well.

Pour into a greased and lined 20-cm (8-in) square cake tin and bake in the centre of a cool oven for about 1 hour, or until firm to the touch.

Meanwhile, to make the rum butter, mix the sugar, nutmeg and rum in a basin. Melt the butter and pour over the other ingredients. Mix well, then pour into a bowl and leave to set. The butter is ready to use, but can be kept in a cool place, well-covered, for several weeks. If you find that it is too sweet for you, reduce the quantity of sugar by about half.

Serve the gingerbread warm, with the rum butter. Rum butter can also be served with oatcakes, oat biscuits (see page 127), Christmas pudding, steamed puddings (see pages 108–9), toasted tea cakes, muffins (see page 126), mincepies, Cumberland rum nicky (see page 113), scones (see page 131) and thinly sliced brown bread, amongst other dishes. (Serves 6–8)

DORSET APPLE AND LEMON TART

*The Potter family used to stay in Lyme Regis sometimes for
their spring holiday. While there in 1904, Beatrix worked
on drawings for* The Tale of Benjamin Bunny. *She wrote
to her editor, Norman Warne, 'There is a splendid view
from this little house. It is at the top of the steep street and
has a nice sunny garden.'*
*Dorset is famous for its apple cakes and puddings and this
apple tart is particularly good.*

For the pastry

125 g (4 oz/¾ cup) plain flour
50 g (2 oz/¼ cup) butter
1 tablespoon caster sugar
1½ (2 US) tablespoons milk

For the filling

2 large cooking apples
50 g (2 oz/¼ cup) sugar
Grated rind and juice of 1 large lemon
2 large eggs

To make the pastry, sieve the flour into a mixing
bowl. Cut the butter into small pieces and rub into
the flour. Dissolve the sugar in the milk, mix into the
flour mixture to form a dough and knead until
smooth. Place in a polythene bag and leave to rest for
30 minutes in the fridge. Roll out thinly on a lightly
floured surface and use to line a 17–20-cm (7–8-in)
loose-bottomed fluted flan tin. Chill in the fridge
again while you prepare the filling.

Pre-heat the oven to 180°C (350°F, gas mark 4).

Peel, core and grate the apples, then add the sugar,
lemon rind and lemon juice and mix well. Beat the
eggs well, add them to the apple mixture and pour
this into the prepared flan case. Bake near the top of a
moderate oven for about 30 minutes, or until the
pastry is well cooked and the topping is golden.
Serve warm or cold with cream, yoghurt or homemade custard. (Serves 4–6)

WESTMORLAND WALNUT AND RAISIN TART

*When Beatrix Potter was seventeen, she
wrote in her journal, 'They cut down the old walnut
up the new road. Poor old tree, I remember it almost as
long as I remember anything hereabouts. They are cutting a
road across the field preparatory to building.
It is the last bit of the orchards left.' Already, she
was aware of the damage being done to the land in the name
of progress. Much later, she fought to preserve
small Lakeland farms and cottages by buying them herself
whenever she could. In her will, Beatrix
left the National Trust over 4,000 acres of land,
including fifteen farms and many cottages, which in 1943
was the largest gift the Trust had ever received.*

For the base

250 g (8 oz) digestive biscuits (or 1⅔ cups graham
cracker crumbs)
100 g (3½ oz/7 tablespoons) butter, melted

For the topping

400 g (14 oz/2⅔ cups) seedless raisins
450 ml (¾ pint/scant 2 cups) boiling water
50 g (2 oz/¼ cup) soft brown sugar
25 g (1 oz/2 tablespoons) butter
40 g (1½ oz) arrowroot
4 (5 US) tablespoons orange juice
125 g (4 oz/1 cup) chopped walnuts

Crush the biscuits finely, then stir in the melted
butter. Line the base of a lightly greased 22.5-cm
(9-in) loose-bottomed flan tin with the biscuit mixture, pressing it down well. Chill in the fridge while
you make the filling.

Pre-heat the oven to 190°C (375°F, gas mark 5).

Simmer the raisins in the boiling water for about 5
minutes, then stir in the sugar and butter. Blend the
arrowroot with the orange juice and add to the raisin
mixture. Cook, stirring until the filling is thick, then

remove from the heat and stir in the nuts. Spread the mixture on to the biscuit base, then bake in a fairly hot oven for 15 minutes. Serve with fresh cream or yoghurt. (Serves 6)

*C*UMBERLAND RUM NICKY

This is a very old traditional Lakeland dish, stemming from the eighteenth century when there was a flourishing trade with the West Indies and the Far East. Wool was exported to these countries for carpet-making, in exchange for spices, brown sugar, molasses and rum. According to local history, the Cumbrian taste for rum came about because, years ago, rum smuggling was rife on this rugged coast. Lakeland folk took 'accidentally broken' casks home with them, rather than let the liquor drip to waste. Rum nicky tends to be a little sickly sweet in its original form for modern palates, especially at the end of a meal, so Jean Butterworth (who used to cook at the White Moss House Hotel on Rydal Water) suggests putting a sharpish apple purée under the dates and rum.

For the pastry

250 g (8 oz/1⅔ cups) plain flour
1 tablespoon icing sugar, sieved
125 g (4 oz/½ cup) butter
1 large egg, beaten

For the filling

3 medium cooking apples
1 heaped tablespoon demerara sugar
125 g (4 oz/⅔ cup) chopped and pitted dates
1 tablespoon cold water
2 (3 US) tablespoons dark rum
50 g (2 oz/¼ cup) butter
2 pieces stem ginger, chopped (optional)
A little milk, to glaze

To make the pastry, sieve the flour with the icing sugar into a mixing bowl. Cut the butter into small pieces and rub into the flour. Add the beaten egg, mix to a firm dough and knead until smooth. Place in a polythene bag and leave to rest in the fridge for 30 minutes.

Meanwhile, peel, core and slice the apples. Place them in a saucepan with the sugar and cook gently until tender. Beat to a smooth purée with a wooden spoon. Place the chopped and stoned dates in a small saucepan with the water. Soften them over a gentle heat, then leave to cool.

Pre-heat the oven to 200°C (400°F, gas mark 6).

Divide the pastry in half and roll out 1 piece on a lightly floured surface. Use to line a 17–20-cm (7–8-in) pie plate or flan dish. Spread the apple purée over the base. Mix the rum with the butter and add to the dates. Stir in the chopped ginger, if using, and spread the mixture over the apple purée.

Roll out the other piece of pastry to make a top for the pie (or make a lattice if you prefer), lightly prick the top, then brush with milk. Bake for 15 minutes, then lower the heat to 180°C (350°F, gas mark 4) and cook for a further 15 minutes, or until the top is golden brown. Serve cut into wedges, hot or cold, with cream or yoghurt. (Serves 6)

Variation

*S*HARROW BAY RUM NICKIES

Use the following mixture when making mince pies instead of mincemeat. Soak 450 g (1 lb/3 cups) currants in 4 (5 US) tablespoons rum for about 1 hour. Melt 125 g (4 oz/½ cup) rum butter (see page 111) with 125 g (4 oz/½ cup) butter, add 2 teaspoons grated nutmeg and the currant mixture. Cool, then use as required.

DAMSON FOOL IN BRANDY-SNAP BASKETS

*I was treated to this delicious pudding the
first night I stayed at Gillian Fletcher's, a small,
extremely friendly guest-house. (It used to be the home
of Farmer Postlethwaite, who appears in* The Tale of
Samuel Whiskers *as 'Farmer Potatoes'.)
The damsons she used were from the nearby town
of Hawkshead, but they are grown all over this part of
Lakeland and we know Beatrix Potter had damson trees in
her orchard at Hill Top.
The combination of rather sharp damson
purée and sweet brandy-snap is excellent.
Although the brandy-snap baskets have to be handled
carefully, there is enough mixture in the recipe for a few
mistakes! Many other fruit fools may be
used if damsons are not available, but don't
add too much sugar or honey.*

For the fool

450 g (1 lb) damsons
2 (3 US) tablespoons cold water
Caster sugar or honey to taste
150 ml (¼ pint/⅔ cup) double cream
150 ml (¼ pint/⅔ cup) natural yoghurt
Sprigs of fresh mint or fresh flowers, to decorate

For the brandy-snap baskets

50 g (2 oz/¼ cup) unsalted butter
50 g (2 oz/¼ cup) demerara sugar
50 g (2 oz/¼ cup) golden syrup
50 g (2 oz/⅓ cup) plain flour
Pinch of salt
½ teaspoon ground ginger
Finely grated rind of ½ a lemon
1 teaspoon brandy

Wash the damsons and remove any stalks. Cook very gently with the water for about 15 minutes, or until very tender. Stir in sugar or honey to taste, then rub through a nylon sieve to make a smooth purée.

To make the brandy-snap baskets, gently heat the butter, sugar and golden syrup until the butter has melted and the sugar has dissolved. Remove from the heat and leave to cool slightly. Sieve the flour, salt and ginger together, then stir into the melted mixture with the lemon rind and brandy, mixing well.

Pre-heat the oven to 170 °C (325 °F, gas mark 3).

Thoroughly grease 2 or 3 large baking trays. (Each batch of biscuits needs to be cooked on a cool baking tray.) Drop heaped tablespoonfuls of the mixture on to a tray, leaving plenty of room for the biscuits to spread. Bake near the top of a moderate oven for 7–8 minutes, or until golden brown. Leave the biscuits on the tray for 2–3 minutes to harden a little, then quickly remove with a palette knife and mould over the bottom of an apple, or an orange. When set in shape, remove from the moulds and cool on wire racks.

Cook the remaining biscuits in the same way. (If any biscuits should set before they have been shaped, return them to the oven for a few minutes to soften again, then reshape them and cool.) Store the brandy-snap baskets in an airtight container for up to 3 days.

To make the fool, whip the cream until it stands in soft peaks. In another bowl, beat the yoghurt until smooth, then fold it into the whipped cream until the mixture is thoroughly blended and very thick. Fold the damson purée into the cream mixture and taste for sweetness. Keep in the fridge until needed.

About 15 minutes before serving, place a brandy-snap basket on each plate and fill with damson fool. Decorate with sprigs of mint or a few tiny flowers from the garden. (Serves 6)

Damson fool in brandy-snap baskets and Sawrey rhubarb and apricot pie, two delicious sweets served at High Green Gate guest-house in Near Sawrey

SAWREY RHUBARB AND APRICOT PIE

*When Beatrix Potter was out in the fields
in hot weather, she was sometimes to be seen
wearing a rhubarb leaf on her head, just like little
Timmy Willie sheltering under a strawberry leaf in* The
Tale of Johnny Town-Mouse. *When the
weather was bad, she would wrap a sack around her
shoulders, like so many other farmers.
This super pudding was invented by Gillian Fletcher for
her guests at High Green Gate in Sawrey.*

For the pastry

175 g (6 oz/1¼ cups) plain flour
Pinch of salt
125 g (4 oz/½ cup) butter
2 teaspoons caster sugar
1 large egg yolk
Cold water, to mix

For the filling

2 (3 US) tablespoons apricot jam, sieved
40 g (1½ oz/3 US tablespoons) butter or margarine
40 g (1½ oz/3 US tablespoons) soft light brown sugar
1 large egg, beaten
40 g (1½ oz/⅓ cup) self-raising flour
½ teaspoon ground ginger
¼ teaspoon ground cinnamon
250 g (8 oz) rhubarb, cooked in the oven with a little
syrup or honey
Crystallised primroses, to decorate (see page 170)
A little icing sugar, for dredging

To make the pastry, sieve the flour and salt together
into a mixing bowl. Cut the butter into small pieces,
then rub into the flour with your fingertips. Stir in
the sugar and mix well.

Beat the egg yolk with 1 tablespoon water and mix
into the pastry with a palette knife. Stir in sufficient
cold water to make a fairly stiff dough. Knead lightly,
then place in a polythene bag and leave to relax in the
fridge for at least 30 minutes. Roll out the pastry on a
lightly floured surface and use to line a 20 cm (8 in)
flan tin. Spread the sieved apricot jam over the base
of the pastry case and chill in the fridge while
making the filling.

Pre-heat the oven to 200°C (400°F, gas mark 6).

Place a baking tray in the oven to heat. Cream the
butter or margarine and sugar together until light
and fluffy, then gradually beat in the egg, a little at a
time. Sieve the flour with the ginger and cinnamon
and fold into the creamed mixture.

Drain the cooked rhubarb well and arrange it over
the jam in the pastry case. Spread the sponge mixture
over the top and bake on the heated baking tray for
10 minutes, then reduce the oven temperature to
180°C (350°F, gas mark 4) and cook for a further 20
minutes, or until the sponge is firm and golden
brown.

Decorate with crystallised primroses and serve
warm or cold with a little icing sugar dredged over
the top. Accompany with homemade custard, cream,
yoghurt or fromage frais. (Serves 6)

From The Tale of Johnny Town-Mouse

*B*LACKCURRANT AND MEADOWSWEET SNOW

*Beatrix Potter was very fond of
blackcurrants and planted blackcurrant, whitecurrant
and redcurrant bushes amongst the lilies, azaleas, phlox
and other old-fashioned flowers in her cottage garden at
Hill Top. She wrote to Millie Warne soon
after buying the farm, telling her of a proposed
visit to a nursery at Windermere 'to choose some bushes'.
Meadowsweet, like angelica and sweet
cicely, can be cooked with fruit to reduce the
amount of sugar needed. It is a lovely plant with the
sweet smell of summer. After William Gaskell's death,
Beatrix wrote movingly in her journal of
her dearest childhood friend, who spent many
holidays with the Potters in Scotland. 'He is sitting
comfortably in the warm sunshine on the
doorstep at Dalguise . . . A little girl in a print
frock and striped stockings [Beatrix herself] bounds to
his side and offers him a bunch of meadowsweet.'*

450 g (1 lb/1 quart) blackcurrants
2 (3 US) tablespoons Crème de Cassis liqueur, or water
4–6 meadowsweet flower heads (optional)
3 tablespoons (¼ cup) cold water
1 (11-g/½-oz) packet powdered gelatine
or 2 (6-g/¼-oz) envelopes American gelatine
Caster sugar or honey, to taste
300 ml (½ pint/1¼ cups) natural yoghurt
2 large egg whites
50 g (2 oz/¼ cup) caster sugar
6 sprigs of fresh blackcurrants with leaves or
crystallised violets (see page 170), to decorate

Rinse the blackcurrants and strip the berries from the stalks, using a fork. Put the fruit in a saucepan with the Cassis or water and flower heads, if using. Cover with a lid and simmer very gently for about 10 minutes, or until fairly soft.

Put the cold water into a small bowl, sprinkle in the gelatine and leave to soak for 5 minutes. When the fruit is tender, remove the pan from the heat and discard the flower heads. Add the soaked gelatine and stir to dissolve in the hot fruit mixture. Rub the fruit through a nylon sieve to make a thick purée, discarding any skin and seeds that remain in the sieve. Sweeten to taste with sugar or honey, then leave the purée to cool until it begins to show signs of setting. Stir the yoghurt until creamy, then fold into the purée.

In a separate bowl, whisk the egg whites until they stand in soft peaks. Add the caster sugar and whisk until glossy, then fold roughly into the blackcurrant mixture to give a marbled effect. Taste to make sure the mixture is sweet enough, stirring in a little extra sugar if necessary.

Turn into a pretty serving bowl or individual tall glasses and chill for several hours until completely set. Decorate with sprigs of blackcurrants and blackcurrant leaves or with crystallised violets, and serve with homemade shortbread or other small biscuits. (Serves 6)

TULLYTHWAITE APRICOT CREAMS

*Beatrix Potter frequently visited her uncle
and aunt at Gwaynynog, their delightful old house
set in a rambling garden in North Wales. She described
the garden there in her journal. 'The garden is very large,
two-thirds surrounded by a red-brick wall
with many apricots, and an inner circle of old
grey apple trees on wooden espaliers. She was later to set*
The Tale of The Flopsy Bunnies *in this very garden.
This lovely recipe from Tullythwaite House
in the village of Underbarrow will not disappoint
the apricot lover. The creams can be made earlier in the
day and re-heated very successfully for serving.*

For the creams

450 g (1 lb) fresh apricots or 250 g (8 oz) dried
apricots, soaked overnight*
Juice of 2 oranges
Pared rind of 1 lemon
50 g (2 oz/¼ cup) caster sugar
A little Cointreau or orange liqueur (optional)
450 ml (¾ pint/scant 2 cups) single cream
3 large eggs
1 egg yolk
1 tablespoon caster sugar
½ (1 US) teaspoon vanilla essence

For the meringue topping

2 large egg whites
125 g (4 oz/½ cup) caster sugar

*If using dried apricots, soak them overnight in the orange juice, lemon rind and enough water to cover. Next day, add the sugar and poach gently until soft.

If using fresh apricots, halve them and remove the stones. Poach gently until soft with the orange juice, lemon rind and sugar. Strain off most of the liquid and reserve. Discard the lemon rind. Liquidise or sieve the fruit and add as much of the poaching liquor as needed to make a spreadable purée. A little orange liqueur may be added at this stage, if you wish.

Pre-heat the oven to 170°C (325°F, gas mark 3).

Put the cream in a saucepan and bring to the boil. Beat the eggs and the egg yolk in a bowl with the sugar and vanilla essence. Pour on the cream and mix well. Strain the mixture into 6 individual ramekins or small ovenproof dishes. Place these in a shallow ovenproof dish or roasting tin half-filled with hot water, and bake in a slow oven for about 20 minutes, or until just firm. Remove from the oven and leave to cool. When cool, cover the surface of the creams evenly with the apricot purée.

To make the meringue, whisk the egg whites in a large bowl until they form soft peaks, then whisk the caster sugar into them, a dessertspoonful at a time, until the mixture is shiny and stiff. Pile or pipe the meringue on top of the apricot purée on each of the creams and bake for a further 15 minutes to set the meringue. Serve warm with small almond biscuits or shortbread. (Serves 6)

Right: Apricot creams photographed at Tullythwaite House, the beautiful country restaurant run by Janet and Michael Greenwood, pictured below with some of their speciality preserves (see page 159)

ELDERFLOWER FRITTERS WITH GOOSEBERRY PURÉE

For the fritters

12 elderflower heads
125 g (4 oz/¾ cup) plain white or wholemeal flour
Pinch of salt
2 (3 US) tablespoons sunflower or safflower oil
150 ml (¼ pint/⅔ cup) dry white wine
Oil, for deep frying
1 large egg white
Icing sugar, for dredging

For the gooseberry purée

450 g (1 lb) green gooseberries, topped and tailed
6 tablespoons (½ cup) dry white wine
1 elderflower head
About 2 (3 US) tablespoons honey

Rinse the elderflower heads and shake them dry in a clean tea-towel. To make the batter, sieve the flour with the salt into a bowl and make a well in the centre. Pour in the oil and the wine, then gradually beat into the dry ingredients to make a smooth, creamy batter. Leave to stand until ready to cook the fritters.

Put the gooseberries in a saucepan with the wine and the elderflower head. Cover with a lid and simmer very gently for about 15 minutes, or until very soft. Remove and discard the elderflower head, then rub the gooseberries through a nylon sieve into a clean pan. Stir in the honey to taste and keep the purée warm until ready to serve.

When ready to cook the fritters, whisk the egg white until stiff and fold into the prepared batter to make it extra light. Heat a pan of deep oil to 180 °C (350 °F). Dip each elderflower head into the batter by holding the stalk, then deep fry two at a time for a few minutes, until crisp and golden brown. Drain well on crumpled kitchen paper and keep hot in the oven until all the flower heads are cooked. (Do not cover them or they will lose their delicious crispness.)

Serve the fritters piping hot, dredged with a little icing sugar, and hand around the warm gooseberry purée separately to spoon over them. (Serves 6)

REDCURRANT AND RASPBERRY ICE CREAM

This is a very fresh-tasting ice-cream made with uncooked redcurrants and raspberries, both of which were grown by Beatrix Potter in the garden of Hill Top. Some of the cream has been replaced by yoghurt, to give a lighter result with fewer calories!

250 g (8 oz/1 pint) redcurrants
250 g (8 oz/1 pint) raspberries
Icing sugar, sieved
Juice of ½ lemon
150 ml (¼ pint/⅔ cup) double cream
150 ml (¼ pint/⅔ cup) natural yoghurt
6 frosted redcurrant sprigs, to decorate

Rinse the redcurrants and strip the berries from the stems, using a fork. Pick over the raspberries, but don't wash them. Blend the fruit in a blender or food processor, then press through a nylon sieve to make a smooth purée. Sweeten with a little sieved icing sugar, then stir in the lemon juice.

Pour the double cream into a large mixing bowl and beat until very thick. Add the yoghurt and beat again until the mixture is well blended, then gently fold in the fruit purée. Pour into a plastic container and place, uncovered, in the freezer. As the mixture freezes around the edges, beat well with a fork until uniformly smooth and creamy again, then leave to freeze for several hours without stirring until firm. Cover with the container lid for storing.

Transfer the ice-cream to the fridge 30 minutes before serving to soften slightly and develop its full flavour. Scoop into chilled glasses and decorate with frosted redcurrant sprigs. (Serves 6)

FLOPSY BUNNIES' SUMMER ICE-CREAM SURPRISE

*The Tale of the Flopsy Bunnies was set
in the rambling country garden of Gwaynynog, the
home of Beatrix's uncle, Fred Burton. It was the sequel to*
The Tale of Peter Rabbit *and* The
Tale of Benjamin Bunny, *and was published in
July 1909. Beatrix had sketched the garden many times
since her first visit nearly fourteen years before.
Tom and Janie Smith, descendants of Beatrix Potter's
uncle and aunt, still live at Gwaynynog and make very
special ice-cream in what was originally the laundry of the
house. The grounds have changed little since poor Cousin
Flopsy went searching for her missing babies. It is still
possible to stand where Flopsy stood and see the same wall,
though obviously trees and shrubs have grown
considerably since Beatrix Potter's day. The garden is now
on view to the public.
Denbigh Farmhouse Ices make 30 flavours of ice-cream and
this special sundae recipe was invented by Mrs Joan
Griffiths from the farm shop.*

Lettuce leaves, to decorate
600 ml (1 pint/2½ cups) blackcurrant ice-cream
600 ml (1 pint/2½ cups) strawberry ice-cream
600 ml (1 pint/2½ cups) mint chocolate chip ice-cream
Chocolate sauce
Chopped hazelnuts
12 fresh strawberries, halved, to decorate
Mint leaves, to decorate
Sugar curls, to decorate

Decorate 6 small plates with a few lettuce leaves and stand 6 tall sundae glasses in the middle of each plate. Fill the glasses with a scoop each of blackcurrant, strawberry and mint chocolate chip ice-cream. Pour a little chocolate sauce on top of the ice-cream and sprinkle the chopped nuts on the chocolate sauce.

Decorate with halved strawberries, mint leaves and sugar curls. (Serves 6)

WILD STRAWBERRY SYLLABUB

450 g (1 lb/1 quart) wild or small garden strawberries
4 tablespoons (⅓ cup) orange liqueur
1 tablespoon clear honey
300 ml (½ pint/1¼ cups) double cream
150 ml (¼ pint/⅔ cup) natural yoghurt
Twists of orange peel, to decorate
Sprigs of strawberry leaves and flowers, to decorate

Place most of the strawberries in a bowl, reserving a few for decoration. Pour over the orange liqueur and the honey and leave to steep for several hours.

Strain the liquid from the strawberries into a measuring jug. Pour 150 ml (¼ pint/⅔ cup) of the liquid into a bowl, add the double cream and whisk until just stiff. (Be careful not to overbeat, or the syllabub will curdle and separate into a buttery mess.) Fold in the yoghurt, then taste and adjust sweetness, if necessary, with a little more honey.

Divide the marinaded strawberries and a little of the left-over juice between 6 glasses. Cover with the syllabub mixture and chill in the fridge before serving. Serve decorated with tiny twists of orange peel, the reserved strawberries and the sprigs of strawberry leaves and flowers. (Serves 6)

From The Tale of The Flopsy Bunnies

Bread, Cakes and Biscuits

WHOLEMEAL SUNFLOWER BREAD

As a child Beatrix was very fond of her paternal grandmother, Jessie Potter, and frequently visited her at Camfield Place in Hertfordshire (now the home of novelist Barbara Cartland). She described it later as 'the place I love best in the world', revelling in the freedom of the countryside and the fresh country food. One of her joys was the homemade bread. She remembered it in her journal, 'It may have been heavy but it never kept me awake and as to tough crust (dusted with flour) why in those days we had teeth.'

This particular recipe does not give soft, delicate bread, but rather a strong and chewy variety with plenty of munchy seeds (which of course you can omit if you prefer).

About 1 tablespoon black treacle
18 g (¾ oz) fresh yeast (25 g [1 oz] if it has been frozen for a while) or 2 (¼-oz) pkgs US active dry yeast
450 ml (¾ pint/scant 2 cups) warm water
700 g (1½ lb/5 cups) wholemeal flour
1½–2 teaspoons sea salt
125–175 g (4–6 oz/⅔–1 cup) sunflower seeds
A little milk, to glaze
Extra sunflower seeds, for sprinkling

Blend the treacle and yeast with the warm water in a small bowl. Leave in a warm place for up to 10 minutes until frothy. Warm a large mixing bowl or the bowl of a mixer or food processor and put in the flour and salt. Pour in the yeast mixture, followed by the roughly crushed sunflower seeds, then mix well with a wooden spoon, a dough hook or a food processor. Knead for about 10 minutes by hand, or a few minutes with a dough hook or processor, until smooth and elastic. Cover the dough with a clean cloth and leave in a warm place for about 1 hour, or until doubled in size.

Lightly butter 2 (450-g/1-lb) loaf tins. Knock back the risen dough (to expel the air so the dough can rise more evenly again) and shape into 2 loaves. Place in the prepared tins, cover with a clean cloth and leave in a warm place for a further 20–30 minutes to double in size again.

Pre-heat the oven to 200 °C (400 °F, gas mark 6).

Brush the top of the loaves with a little milk and sprinkle with sunflower seeds. Bake near the top of a fairly hot oven for 30–35 minutes, or until the loaves sound hollow when tapped with your knuckles. Turn out on to a wire cooling rack and leave to cool. (If you want the outside of the loaves to be on the soft side, cover immediately with a dampened tea towel so that the steam given off softens the crust.) This bread keeps very well and freezes beautifully. (Makes 2 [450-g/1-lb] loaves)

Variations

Other seeds, such as sesame, pumpkin and poppy, may be added or mixed with the sunflower seeds, to your own taste. You could also substitute one or two of the following for the sunflower seeds: 75 g (3 oz/½ cup) sultanas or raisins; coarsely grated carrot, apple or fennel; roughly chopped dried banana flakes; 150 g (5 oz/1 cup) roughly chopped nuts.

HERBY SODA BREAD

Oats are one of the few crops able to withstand the cold, damp upland areas of the north of England and Scotland. Beatrix Potter mentions 'the bonny barley and oats up north!' During her holidays in the Lake District, she drove past the patches of oats grown for oatmeal to make the 'havver' or 'clap bread', still the bread most widely made in rural areas of Cumbria. The name 'havver' comes from the Old Norse 'hafrar', meaning oats, and 'clap' because the bread was clapped between the hands to make it thin. It was baked on a circular iron griddle or 'backstone'.

This recipe for soda bread includes some rolled oats and is a good loaf to make if you are in a hurry. Soda bread is always best eaten as fresh as possible.

Eleanor Quinlan at the Mill Hotel, Mungrisdale, serves a very similar herb soda bread with her casserole of venison described on page 75.

124

450 g (1 lb/3½ cups) plain wholemeal flour
125 g (4 oz/¾ cup) plain white flour
50 g (2 oz/½ cup) rolled oats
1 teaspoon bicarbonate of soda
1 teaspoon salt
2 (3 US) tablespoons chopped fresh parsley
3 tablespoons (¼ cup) chopped fresh herbs, such as
thyme, marjoram, sage, chives, mint or rosemary,
or 3 teaspoons dried herbs
About 450 ml (¾ pint/scant 2 cups) buttermilk, sour
milk or a mixture of half milk and half yoghurt

Pre-heat the oven to 230 °C (450 °F, gas mark 8).

Place all the dry ingredients, including the herbs, in a large bowl and mix together. Make a well in the centre and pour in enough liquid to mix to a soft, but not sticky, dough. Knead very gently for about 1 minute, then shape into a large round loaf about 5 cm (2 in) thick. Place on a greased and floured baking tray and cut a deep cross on top.

Bake near the top of a hot oven for 15 minutes, then reduce the temperature to 200 °C (400 °F, gas mark 6) and bake for a further 20–25 minutes, or until the loaf sounds hollow when tapped on the bottom.

Cool on a wire rack for about 15 minutes before eating slightly warm. (If you don't like a very crisp crust, wrap the loaf in a clean tea-towel while it cools, so that the steam given off softens the crust a little.) The bread is delicious served with homemade soup or cheese. Made without herbs it can be served warm with homemade jam, lemon curd or honey and cream for tea. (Makes 1 large loaf)

SAGE AND ONION GRANARY STICK

This bread is ideal for a picnic. It is also good served warm with homemade soup, cheese or potted meat and fish.

12 g (½ oz) fresh yeast or 1½ teaspoons dried yeast
or 1 (¼-oz) pkg US active dry yeast
300 ml (½ pint/1¼ cups) warm water
Pinch of sugar

25 g (1 oz/2 US tablespoons) butter
1 large onion, finely chopped
450 g (1 lb/3½ cups) granary flour or any wholemeal
flour
1 teaspoon sea salt
Freshly milled black pepper
2 (3 US) tablespoons chopped fresh sage
or 2 teaspoons dried
A little milk, to glaze
Fine oatmeal, for sprinkling

Blend the fresh yeast with the warm water and sugar in a bowl; if using dried yeast, sprinkle it into the warm water with the sugar. Leave in a warm place for 15 minutes, until frothy. Meanwhile, melt the butter in a small saucepan and cook the onion gently until soft and transparent, but not brown. Put the flour, salt, a little black pepper and the herbs into a large mixing bowl. Mix together, then make a well in the centre. Add the onion mixture and the yeast liquid. Beat together thoroughly until the dough leaves the sides of the bowl clean.

Turn on to a lightly floured surface and knead well for about 10 minutes by hand, or a few minutes only with a dough hook or processor, until smooth and elastic. Place the dough in an oiled polythene bag and leave in a warm place for about 1 hour, or until doubled in size.

Turn the dough on to a floured surface again and knead lightly. Shape into a sausage shape about 40 cm (16 in) long and place on a greased baking tray. Slash the top several times with a knife, then cover and leave in a warm place for a further 30 minutes or until doubled in size again.

Pre-heat the oven to 230 °C (450 °F, gas mark 8).

Brush the top of the loaf with a little milk and sprinkle with some fine oatmeal. Bake near the top of a hot oven for 10 minutes, then reduce the temperature to 200 °C (400 °F, gas mark 6) and bake for a further 15–20 minutes.

Remove from the oven and leave to cool on a wire rack. (Makes 1 large French stick)

'DEAR LITTLE MUFFINS'

*In Victorian and Edwardian London, the
'muffin man', carrying his wares on a large tray
skilfully balanced on his flat hat, was one of the most
popular street vendors. He would announce his arrival
around 4 pm with a large brass handbell.
Surely he must have livened up many Sunday afternoons
at Number 2 Bolton Gardens for the young
Beatrix and Bertram. Both muffins and crumpets
must have found their way into the nursery at teatime, to
be toasted on long brass forks in front of the open fire.
Muffins certainly appear many times in Beatrix's books.
Muffins made with unbleached flour,
stoneground at Muncaster Mill near Waberthwaite
in Eskdale, are a speciality of Sheila's Cottage. This is
a delightful restaurant in Ambleside. It was Egon Ronay's
'Tea Place of The Year' in 1988 and won a
Tea Council Award of Excellence in 1990. Stewart
and Janice Greaves have been running Sheila's Cottage
for nearly twenty years and have made it into somewhat of
a shrine for afternoon tea. Their
scrumptious muffins are baked to this recipe in
the restaurant kitchen and served hot at 3pm with fresh
cream and black cherry jam.*

Muffins from Sheila's Cottage at Ambleside

25 g (1 oz) fresh yeast or 2 (¼-oz) pkgs US active dry
yeast
1 teaspoon caster sugar
225–275 ml (8–10 fl oz/1–1¼ cups) warm water
450 g (1 lb/3½ cups) unbleached plain white flour
1 rounded teaspoon salt

Blend the yeast, sugar and warm water together in a small bowl and leave in a warm place for 10 minutes, or until frothy. Sieve the flour and salt together into a large mixing bowl. Add the yeast liquid and mix with a fork to form a soft dough. Turn out on to a lightly floured surface and knead for about 10 minutes by hand, or work with a dough hook or in a processor for a few minutes until the dough is smooth. Place the dough in a large oiled plastic bag and leave to rise in a warm place for 1–1½ hours, or until it has doubled in size. Knock back to expel the air so the dough can rise more evenly a second time and knead again for about 5 minutes until it is smooth and firm.

Roll out the dough to about 12 mm (½ in) thick, cover it with a tea towel and leave to relax for a further 10 minutes. Cut into rounds with a 7.5-cm (3-in) plain cutter. Dust a baking tray with flour, then place the muffins on it and dust them with flour. Put the tray inside the oiled plastic bag and leave in a warm place for 30–40 minutes until the muffins have risen and doubled in volume.

Pre-heat the oven to 230 °C (450 °F, gas mark 8).

Bake the muffins for about 10 minutes, turning over carefully after 5 minutes. Cool on a wire rack.

To serve in the traditional way, break them just a little around their 'waists' without opening them, then toast lightly on both sides. To eat, pull them apart without cutting and butter generously, or spread with cream and jam. (Makes about 12)

*B*UTTERED OAT BISCUITS

Many Lakelanders believe that a good plate of 'poddish', or porridge, made from freshly milled oatmeal, keeps the doctor away. The villagers who remember Beatrix Potter say that she always had a bowl of porridge for breakfast, and she certainly grew oats on the farm. Mollie Green, who is in her eighties, serves the most delicious buttered oat biscuits with morning coffee at her cottage in Near Sawrey, but she won't part with the recipe until she retires! Try this recipe instead.

125 g (4 oz/¾ cup) plain white or wholemeal flour
½ teaspoon salt
½ teaspoon bicarbonate of soda
125 g (4 oz/1¼ cups) rolled or porridge oats
75 g (3 oz/6 US tablespoons) butter or margarine
75 g (3 oz/6 US tablespoons) lard
75 g (3 oz/6 US tablespoons) caster sugar
3–4 (4–5 US) tablespoons milk

Pre-heat the oven to 200 °C (400 °F, gas mark 6).

Sieve the flour with the salt and bicarbonate of soda into a mixing bowl, then stir in the oats. Cut the fat into small pieces and rub into the flour mixture. Stir in the sugar and add the milk gradually to mix to a firmish dough.

Roll out on a lightly floured board to about 3 mm (⅛ in) thick. Cut into rounds using a 6-cm (2½-in) plain cutter and place on a lightly greased baking tray. (These biscuits don't spread during cooking, so they can be arranged close together.) Bake near the top of a fairly hot oven for about 10 minutes, or until pale golden brown. Cool on a wire rack.

Spread with plenty of butter and serve either on their own, or with soft cheese, a good-flavoured hard cheese, or with homemade jam, lemon curd, honey or marmalade. Oat biscuits are often served with rum butter in Lakeland (see page 111). (Makes about 20)

Mollie Green in her own tea-room in Near Sawrey, where she provides visitors with delicious home-baked cakes and biscuits

LEMON CHEESE TANTADLIES

The visitor to Near Sawrey can still take tea in Mollie Green's front-parlour at Anvil Cottage, opposite the building which appears as the village shop in The Tale of Ginger and Pickles. _Mollie has lived and worked in this picturesque cottage since 1911 and knew Beatrix Potter. It was Mollie's mother who started the bakery business in the cottage, producing delicious homemade bread, tea-cakes, scones, muffins, biscuits, pies, vanilla slices and plum cakes. Her lemon cheese cakes, 'tantadlies', were especially popular. They were given this extraordinary name by Farmer Postlethwaite (Farmer Potatoes in_ The Tale of Samuel Whiskers) _who used this word for cakes that 'went everywhere when you bit into them!'_
This recipe uses rich shortcrust pastry to reduce the amount of pastry and make them easier to eat!

For the pastry

250 g (8 oz/1⅔ cups) plain flour
Pinch of salt
3 tablespoons (¼ cup) icing sugar
175 g (6 oz/¾ cup) unsalted butter
1 large egg
1 egg yolk

For the filling

4 large eggs
175 g (6 oz/¾ cup) caster sugar or honey
150 ml (¼ pint/⅔ cup) double cream
Finely grated rind and juice of 2 large lemons
A little icing sugar, for dredging
Crystallised primroses or violets, to decorate (see page 170)

To make the pastry, sieve the flour, salt, and sugar together into a mixing bowl. Rub in the butter lightly with your fingertips until the mixture resembles fine breadcrumbs. Beat together the egg and the egg yolk, then stir into the mixture with a fork. With floured fingers, gather the dough into a ball and knead very lightly until smooth. Place in a floured polythene bag and chill in the fridge for at least 30 minutes.

Pre-heat the oven to 190 °C (375 °F, gas mark 5).

Roll out the pastry and use to line well-greased shallow 6-cm (2½-in) patty tins. Bake blind for 10 minutes, then remove from the oven and leave to cool.

To make the filling, beat the eggs with the sugar or honey in a heatproof basin until the sugar has completely dissolved. Stir in the cream, followed by the lemon rind and juice. Arrange the basin over a pan of simmering water and stir the mixture until it is as thick as custard. Allow to cool.

Lower the oven temperature to 170 °C (325 °F, gas mark 3), then spoon the lemon filling into the tartlet shells and bake for 5–10 minutes, or until set. Cool on a wire rack. Dredge with a little icing sugar just before serving and decorate with crystallised primroses or violets. (Makes about 18)

HAWKSHEAD SEED WIGS

Small cakes of spiced dough, known as wigs, used to be sold in Hawkshead, like many other Cumbrian villages and towns. They were usually eaten at Christmas, dipped into elderberry wine or mulled ale. The original wigs were made with yeast and were split and spread with rum butter while still warm. This more modern recipe is easier and very tasty. Beatrix was a regular visitor to the little market town of Hawkshead for shopping and business.

250 g (8 oz/1⅔ cups) self-raising flour
½ teaspoon ground nutmeg
75 g (3 oz/6 US tablespoons) caster sugar
125 g (4 oz/½ cup) butter or margarine
50 g (2 oz/⅓ cup) currants
50 g (2 oz/⅓ cup) sultanas
25 g (1 oz) candied peel, chopped
1½ teaspoons caraway seeds
1 standard (medium) egg, beaten
A little milk, to mix

Pre-heat the oven to 220 °C (425 °F, gas mark 7).

Sieve the flour with the nutmeg into a mixing bowl. Stir in the sugar, then lightly rub in the fat until the mixture resembles breadcrumbs. Stir in the dried fruit, peel and caraway seeds, then mix to a stiff dough with the egg, adding a little milk if necessary.

Using two forks, place small heaps of the mixture on a greased baking tray, allowing plenty of room for expansion during cooking. Bake near the top of a hot oven for about 15 minutes, or until golden brown and firm. Leave to cool a little before removing from the baking tray to a wire rack.

Serve warm from the oven, either plain or split and spread with plain butter or Cumberland rum butter (see page 111). Seed wigs are very good served with mulled elderberry wine (see page 143) or lambswool (see page 141) at Christmas time. (Makes about 12)

GINGERSNAPS

Beatrix Potter had happy memories of her grandmamma's 'very hard gingersnap biscuits'.

350 g (12 oz/2½ cups) self-raising flour
1 rounded teaspoon ground ginger
1 teaspoon bicarbonate of soda
125 g (4 oz/½ cup) demerara sugar
125 g (4 oz/½ cup) soft light brown sugar
125 g (4 oz/½ cup) butter or margarine
75 g (3 oz/6 US tablespoons) golden syrup
1 large egg, beaten

Pre-heat the oven to 180 °C (350 °F, gas mark 4).

Sieve the flour, ginger and bicarbonate of soda together into a bowl. Stir in the sugars. Melt the fat very gently with the syrup and pour into the dry ingredients. Mix with the egg to form a dough.

Form into balls about the size of a small walnut and place well apart on a greased baking tray (cook in batches). Flatten them slightly with a fork and bake near the top of a moderate oven for about 10 minutes, until golden brown. (Makes about 45)

SAWREY SHORTBREAD

The idea for this recipe was given to me by Jean Butterworth who, with her husband, used to run the well-known White Moss House Hotel at Rydal Water, near Grasmere. The original recipe was given to Jean 25 years ago by the lady who then served afternoon tea in High Green Gate cottage, Near Sawrey.

For the shortbread

125 g (4 oz/½ cup) butter
50 g (2 oz/⅓ cup) icing sugar, sieved
125 g (4 oz/¾ cup) plain flour
50 g (2 oz/⅓ cup) cornflour
1 teaspoon ground ginger

For the icing

50 g (2 oz/⅓ cup) icing sugar, sieved
2 (3 US) tablespoons cold water
Ground ginger, to taste

Pre-heat the oven to 150 °C (300 °F, gas mark 2).

Pound the butter and icing sugar together a little, until soft. Sieve the flours and ginger together, then work into the butter mixture. Mix lightly until a dough is formed.

Press into a 20-cm (8-in) sandwich tin and prick all over with a fork. Pinch around the edge with your finger and thumb to decorate, then bake at the bottom of a cool oven for about 60 minutes, or until an even pale gold colour. Remove from the oven and leave in the tin to cool. When the shortbread has cooled a little, mark into triangles.

To make the icing, mix the icing sugar and water together. Beat in ginger to taste, then dribble over the cold shortbread. (Makes a 20-cm [8-in] round)

Treacle and buttermilk scones (left) and Lakeland lemon bread (right)

$\mathscr{T}$REACLE AND GINGER BUTTERMILK SCONES

———————

*In her journal, Beatrix writes of a visit
to Ballycock Farm when the Potter family were
staying in Scotland for their annual summer holiday of
1892. 'Miss May Stewart was making scones on a girdle at
the great open fire, with half a tree at
the back of the logs . . . The fire had burnt for
four and twenty years.' Miss Stewart abandoned the scones
to brush her hair before Beatrix photographed her.
Despite this, the scones 'were very good'.
This should give us all encouragement!
Treacle scones are on the menus of many
Lakeland tea-places, spread with rum butter.
Both treacle and ginger have been widely used here since
the eighteenth century, when trade with the
East expanded through the Cumbrian ports of Maryport,
Workington and Whitehaven. Spice cupboards, often built
into the wall alongside the hearth to keep
valuable spices dry, are a special feature of
old Cumbrian buildings.*

250 g (8 oz/1⅔ cups) self-raising flour (white or wholemeal)
1 level teaspoon ground ginger
25 g (1 oz/2 US tablespoons) caster or soft brown sugar
50 g (2 oz/¼ cup) butter or margarine
1 tablespoon black treacle or golden syrup
About 150 ml (¼ pint/⅔ cup) buttermilk, sour milk or fresh milk
Extra milk, to glaze

Pre-heat the oven to 230 °C (450 °C, gas mark 8).

Sieve the flour with the ginger into a mixing bowl, then stir in the sugar. Cut the fat into small pieces and rub lightly into the flour, using just the tips of your fingers. Warm the treacle or golden syrup by placing it in a measuring jug and standing the jug in a basin of hot water. Add sufficient buttermilk, sour milk or fresh milk to make up to 150 ml (¼ pint/⅔ cup) of liquid.

Make a well in the centre of the rubbed-in mixture and pour in the liquid. Quickly mix to a soft, but not sticky, dough. Turn out on to a lightly floured surface and knead very briefly until smooth. Roll or pat out until about 18 mm (¾ in) thick, then, using a 6-cm

(2¼-in) fluted cutter, cut into rounds. Alternatively, cut the dough into triangles with a sharp knife. Place the scones on a lightly greased baking tray and glaze the tops with milk. Bake at the top of a hot oven for 8–10 minutes, until well-risen and golden brown.

Serve warm and spread liberally with butter, rum butter (see page 111) or thick cream. (Makes about 12)

Variations

DEVONSHIRE CREAM TEA SCONES

Omit the ginger and treacle. Mix to a dough with 1 large egg beaten with 3–4 (4–5 US) tablespoons milk. Serve with homemade jam, lemon curd, honey or golden syrup and a dollop of clotted cream.

RICH FRUIT SCONES

Use mixed spice or cinnamon instead of ginger and omit the treacle. Stir 75 g (3 oz/⅔ cup) dried fruit – currants, raisins, sultanas, chopped dates, prunes, apricots or glacé cherries – into the rubbed-in mixture. Mix to a dough with 1 large egg beaten with 3–4

(4–5 US) tablespoons milk or simply 150 ml (¼ pint/ ⅔ cup) milk. (25 g [1 oz/¼ cup] chopped walnuts may also be added.) Serve warm and spread with butter, rum butter or jam and cream.

CHEESE SCONES

Omit the sugar, ginger and treacle, but sieve 1 teaspoon dry English mustard and a large pinch each of celery salt and cayenne pepper, or curry powder, with the flour. Stir 125 g (4 oz/1 cup) grated hard good-flavoured cheese, preferably mature Cheddar, into the rubbed-in mixture. Continue as before, sprinkling the top of the scones with a little extra grated cheese. Butter when warm and serve with vegetable soup and casseroles.

HERB SCONES

Omit the sugar, ginger and treacle. Stir 2 (3 US) tablespoons chopped fresh herbs or 2 teaspoons dried herbs into the rubbed-in mixture. 50 g (2 oz/½ cup) chopped walnuts or grated cheese may also be added. Continue as before. Serve buttered with soups and casseroles.

LAKELAND LEMON BREAD

*Lakelanders are fond of cakes and many
traditional kinds are still made and eaten in Cumbria.
This moist lemon bread is one of them and must have been
eaten many times by Beatrix and her husband.
Traditionally, it is served very fresh, spread with lemon
curd, but the loaf may be iced, if you wish, for a change.*

For the loaf

175 g (6 oz/¾ cup) butter or margarine
300 g (10 oz/1¼ cups) caster sugar
4 eggs, lightly beaten
150 g (5oz/1 cup) self-raising flour
150 g (5 oz/1 cup) plain flour
125 g (4 oz/1 cup) chopped walnuts
Grated rind and juice of 2 large lemons

For the icing (optional)

125 g (4oz/¾ cup) icing sugar
About 2 (3 US) tablespoons lemon juice

Pre-heat the oven to 180 °C (350 °F, gas mark 4).

Cream the butter and sugar together until pale and
fluffy. Gradually mix in the lightly beaten eggs, then
fold in both the flours, followed by the nuts. Finally,
stir in the lemon rind and juice.

Spoon the mixture into a lined and greased 900-g
(2-lb/9 in × 5 in) loaf tin and bake near the top of a
moderate oven for about 1 hour, or until firm to the
touch. Turn out on to a wire rack and leave to cool. If
you wish to ice the loaf, sieve the icing sugar into a
bowl and mix with enough lemon juice to make a
coating consistency. When the loaf is cold, spoon the
icing over the top.

If not iced, serve sliced and buttered, with honey
or homemade lemon curd (see page 161). The bread
also freezes very well. (Makes a 900-g [2-lb] loaf)

Variation

SULTANA AND LEMON BREAD

Substitute sultanas for the chopped walnuts and
make as before.

GRASMERE GINGERBREAD

*The traditional Grasmere gingerbread is still
baked at a tiny shop in the Lakeland village, which
holds about three customers at a time. This quaint building
was originally a school, run by the church
from 1660–1854. When another school was built
after the Education Act was introduced which made
education compulsory, the church allowed the newly
widowed Sarah Nelson and her two daughters to live in the
little cottage. To make ends meet, Sarah
started baking gingerbread for the travellers who
patronised the inn opposite the cottage. She continued
to make and sell her gingerbread until her death in 1904,
aged 88, when the then-flourishing business
was carried on by her two nieces. Today the gingerbread is
still made to the original recipe. It has always been popular
with local people as well as visitors and the shop
is packed with customers from April to November.
Quantities of this very special 'shortbread' are consumed
with other good Cumbrian fare at the
famous Grasmere Sports, held annually on the
nearest Thursday to 20 August since 1852. Beatrix Potter
regularly attended the Sports while holidaying in the Lake
District and later while living at Sawrey. She must have
eaten the gingerbread many times.*

*The original recipe is kept a closely guarded
secret in the National Westminster bank, but this
recipe is characteristically hard in the middle and crumbly
on top and quite delicious.*

250 g (8 oz/1⅔ cups) fine oatmeal, or wholemeal flour
½ teaspoon bicarbonate of soda
½ teaspoon cream of tartar
Pinch of salt
2 rounded teaspoons ground ginger
125 g (4 oz/½ cup) butter
125 g (4 oz/½ cup) soft light brown sugar
1 rounded tablespoon golden syrup
25 g (1 oz) whole candied peel, grated or chopped
very finely

Pre-heat the oven to 170 °C (325 °F, gas mark 3).

Sieve the oatmeal or flour with the bicarbonate of soda, cream of tartar, salt and ginger – adding any bran remaining in the sieve. Put the butter, sugar and syrup into a saucepan and heat very gently until the butter has just melted. Beat into the dry ingredients, which should bind the mixture rather dryly. (Don't be tempted to add any extra liquid.)

Press most of the mixture firmly into a lightly greased shallow 20 cm (8 in) square tin. Scatter with peel, then sprinkle the rest of the gingerbread mixture lightly over the top. Bake near the bottom of a cool oven for 40–50 minutes, or until pale gold in colour.

Remove from the oven and leave in the tin until cold. As the gingerbread is cooling, mark into squares or fingers with a knife. Serve as they are for tea, or as a pudding topped with whipped cream flavoured with a little finely chopped preserved stem ginger and some of the ginger syrup. (See also the recipe for gingerbread with rum butter on page 111.) (Makes enough to fill a 20-cm [8-in] square tin)

From The Tale of The Pie and
The Patty-Pan

BORROWDALE TEABREAD

This rich fruit bread is traditionally served as part of the famous Lakeland farmhouse tea. When Beatrix had married Willie Heelis and was living at Castle Cottage in Near Sawrey, she wrote to a friend, 'I can't do much entertaining at the farm, with farm servants, but we can stand a good farmhouse tea.' Who needs more? The fruit for this loaf needs to be soaked in tea.

450 g (1 lb/3 cups) mixed currants, raisins and
sultanas
300 ml (½ pint/1¼ cups) strong tea
175 g (6 oz/¾ cup) soft brown sugar
1 large egg, well beaten
25 g (1 oz/2 US tablespoons) butter or margarine,
melted
275 g (9 oz/1¾ cups) plain flour
½ teaspoon bicarbonate of soda

Soak the fruit overnight in the tea, in a large mixing bowl.

Pre-heat the oven to 180 °C (350 °F, gas mark 4).

Stir into the soaked fruit the sugar, the egg and the melted fat. Sieve the flour and the bicarbonate of soda into the mixture and mix well. Spoon into a lightly greased and lined 900-g (2-lb/9 in × 5 in) loaf tin and bake in a moderate oven for 1–1¼ hours, or until firm to the touch. Leave in the tin for about 5 minutes, then turn out and cool on a wire rack.

Serve sliced and generously buttered. (Makes a 900-g [2-lb] loaf)

ICED HONEY CAKE

*Shortly after Beatrix had bought her
first Lake District home, Hill Top, she wrote to
tell Millie Warne that she had found a swarm of fine bees,
blown out of a tree near the quarry. 'No
one in the village has lost them, & I don't mean
to inquire further afield! I have bought a box-hive &
Satterthwaite is fixing it up for me.'
The cake has a delicious flavour, which
varies according to the type of honey used.*

For the cake

125 g (4 oz/½ cup) light soft brown or demerara sugar
150 g (5 oz/scant ¾ cup) soft margarine
175 g (6 oz/¾ cup) clear honey
1 tablespoon cold water
2 large eggs
200 g (7 oz/1⅓ cups) self-raising flour, sieved

For the icing

125 g (4 oz/¾ cup) icing sugar
1 tablespoon clear honey
1 tablespoon cold water
Crystallised primroses, to decorate (see page 170)

Pre-heat the oven to 180 °C (350 °F, gas mark 4).

Heat the sugar, margarine, honey and water together in a large saucepan. Remove from the heat when the margarine has melted, then beat in the eggs and the sieved self-raising flour. Whisk thoroughly, then pour into a greased and lined 21 cm (8½ in) round, or 20 cm (8 in) square, cake tin. Bake near the top of a moderate oven for about 40 minutes, or until well risen and firm.

Meanwhile, to make the icing, sieve the icing sugar into a bowl. Mix the honey and water together, then stir into the icing sugar. Pour the icing over the cake while still warm. Leave to cool until the icing is

Left: Coffee and pecan sponge-cake

almost firm, then decorate with crystallised primroses. (Makes a 21-cm [8½-in] round, or a 20-cm [8-in] square, cake)

COFFEE AND PECAN SPONGE-CAKE

*Beatrix Potter bemoans the demise of the
village shop in* The Tale of Ginger and Pickles,
*'a person cannot live on "seed wigs" and sponge-cake
and butter-buns' from the tradesmen's carts. The tiny grocer's
shop in Sawrey with its oak flour chest,
small wooden herb and spice drawers and bacon hanging
from the ceiling, inspired her to write the story, which was
very well received in the village.
I guarantee that this sponge-cake will
be as good as Timothy Baker's!*

For the cake

250 g (8 oz/1 cup) butter or soft margarine
250 g (8 oz/1 cup) caster or soft dark brown sugar
4 standard (medium) eggs
250 g (8 oz/1⅔ cups) self-raising flour, sieved
2 (3 US) tablespoons cold strong coffee or coffee essence
75 g (3 oz/¾ cup) roughly chopped pecans or walnuts

For the icing

175 g (6 oz/1 cup) icing sugar
50 g (2 oz/¼ cup) unsalted butter, softened
3 tablespoons (¼ cup) single cream
2 (3 US) tablespoons cold strong coffee or coffee essence
12 pecan or walnut halves, to decorate

Pre-heat the oven to 180 °C (350 °F, gas mark 4).

Cream the fat and sugar together until light and fluffy. Beat the eggs and add to the creamed mixture a little at a time, beating in well. Gently fold in the sieved flour, the coffee and the nuts.

Divide the mixture between 2 (20-cm/8-in) greased

sandwich tins and bake at the top of a moderate oven for 20–25 minutes, or until well risen and springy to the touch. Remove from the oven and leave to cool in the tins for a few minutes before turning out on to a wire rack.

To make the icing, sieve the icing sugar into a bowl and add the butter. Beat together until light and fluffy, then mix in the cream and the coffee. Sandwich the cooled sponges together with a third of the icing, then spread the rest over the top and down the sides. Decorate with pecan or walnut halves. (Makes a 20-cm [8-in] cake)

RICH CHOCOLATE RUM CAKE

Beatrix Potter certainly enjoyed chocolate. Delmar Banner, a local artist who painted the famous portrait of Beatrix in the National Gallery, visited her at Castle Cottage in 1935 and noticed 'a rather naughty quantity of silver chocolate paper on a little table'! During the Second World War, Beatrix's many American friends kept her supplied with chocolate. In 1942, she wrote to Bertha Mahoney Miller, 'I eat your chocolate at the moment. We are getting a fair amount of chocolate here, but it does not taste very nice.'
There was a p.s. – 'The chocolate is good!'
This chocolate cake is also good; very moist and rich with a fudgey icing, which is really gilding the lily. For a plainer cake, serve the cake without icing, or spread with fresh cream for a pudding.

For the cake

300 g (10 oz/2 cups) self-raising flour
½ teaspoon salt
35 g (1¼ oz/¼ cup) cocoa
1 teaspoon bicarbonate of soda
175 g (6 oz/¾ cup) caster or soft dark brown sugar
150 g (5 oz/¾ cup) butter or margarine
200 g (7 oz/½ cup) golden syrup
300 ml (½ pint/1¼ cups) milk
½ (1 US) teaspoon vanilla essence
About 2 (3 US) tablespoons rum (optional)

For the icing

75 g (3 oz/scant ½ cup) soft brown sugar
120 ml (4 fl oz/½ cup) evaporated milk
75 g (3 oz) plain chocolate
40 g (1½ oz/3 US tablespoons) butter
Crystallised flowers or herbs (see page 170), or nuts and glacé fruit, to decorate

Pre-heat the oven to 180 °C (350 °F, gas mark 4).

Sieve the flour, salt, cocoa and bicarbonate of soda into a large bowl, then stir in the sugar. Put the fat, syrup and milk into a saucepan and melt over a very gentle heat. Beat into the dry ingredients very gradually to avoid lumps forming, then mix in the vanilla essence.

Pour into a greased and lined 20 cm (8 in) round, deep cake tin and bake near the top of a moderate oven for about 1¼ hours or until the cake is firm to the touch. Cool slightly before removing from the tin on to a wire rack.

To make the icing, put the sugar and evaporated milk in a heavy saucepan and stir well. Heat gently to dissolve the sugar, stirring frequently. When the sugar has completely dissolved, bring to the boil. Simmer over a very low heat for 6 minutes without stirring. Remove the pan from the heat, then break up the chocolate and add it to the pan. Stir to dissolve the chocolate, then stir in the butter. When it is cool, cover with cling film and chill until it is thick.

When the cake is completely cold, split in two and sprinkle the rum over the cut surface. Spread with half of the chocolate icing and sandwich the two halves together. Swirl the remaining icing over the top of the cake and decorate with crystallised flowers or herbs, or with nuts and glacé fruit. (Makes a 20-cm [8-in] round cake)

*W*ESTMORLAND PEPPER CAKE

*Beatrix's husband Willie Heelis enjoyed
country dancing, and during the revival of folk-dancing
which swept the Lake District after the First World War, he
danced with the village team. He would
drive his Bradbury motorbike to local dances,
and later transported other members of the team in
the new Morris Cowley that replaced it. Sometimes Beatrix
went along too, for she was enchanted by
the dancing and all that went with it. 'The Morris
bells and baldricks! The plum cake and laughter.' In
winter, the dancers gathered in the school at Far Sawrey
and in the summer, danced out in the open
air. Several of the villagers of Sawrey still remember
dancing in the upstairs room at Hill Top and the pretty
floral print dresses that Beatrix and Willie
bought for the local team.*

*Pepper cakes have been well-loved in the
North since the eighteenth century, when allspice was
imported and used in cake-making. This spicy flavouring
was also known as Jamaican Pepper, hence
the name. The recipe which follows is similar to the
plum cake eaten at the local folk-dancing
events which Beatrix so enjoyed.*

125 g (4 oz/½ cup) demerara sugar
125 g (4 oz/¾ cup) currants
150 g (5 oz/¾ cup) raisins
150 g (5 oz/¾ cup) sultanas
75 g (3 oz) glacé cherries (preferably naturally
coloured)
125 g (4 oz/½ cup) butter or margarine
Pinch of salt
300 ml (½ pint/1¼ cups) cold water
1 large egg, beaten
300 g (10 oz/2 cups) self-raising flour
1 teaspoon mixed spice
¼ teaspoon freshly grated nutmeg
¼ teaspoon ground black pepper
Juice of 1 small orange
50 g (2 oz/⅓ cup) whole blanched almonds

Put the sugar, dried fruit, cherries, butter or margarine, salt and water in a large saucepan. Bring to the boil and simmer gently for 20 minutes. Leave to cool for about 15 minutes.

Pre-heat the oven to 170°C (325°F, gas mark 3).

Stir the beaten egg into the cooled fruit mixture. Sieve the flour with the spices and add to the mixture. Mix well and add sufficient orange juice to make a soft dropping consistency.

Spoon into a greased and lined 20-cm (8-in) round deep cake tin. Level the cake and arrange the almonds on top. Bake in the centre of a moderate oven for about 1½ hours, or until cooked. (Test by inserting a skewer into the middle; if the skewer comes out clean the cake is ready.) Cool on a wire rack.

Serve with chunks of Wensleydale, Cheshire or Lancashire cheese and maybe a nip of damson or sloe gin. (Makes a 20-cm [8-in] round cake)

Mice enjoy a 'dance supper party' in The Fairy Caravan

Drinks and Sweets

DAMSON GIN

*Lakeland cooks specialise in making both
damson gin and wine. In her journal, Beatrix Potter
recalls her visit to Wray Castle on the west side of Lake
Windermere, in 1896. 'Down in the scullery
of the great kitchen, Jane [the cook] had a clothes-basket
full of elder-berries for wine, some greeny-white, a variety I
never saw. She had already made damson
wine and ginger, and outside was a litter of walnuts
blown down by the gale. It is a season for wild fruits, haws
on the bushes as red-over as red hawthorn
in spring, crabs and wild bullaces, little sound amber
plums, and blackberries, more than I ever
saw except at Coniston.'
I am sure Jane must have made damson gin
as well. A rich, dark red and extremely potent cold-weather
tipple, it is just right for drinking at
Christmas and the New Year. The herbs pennyroyal
(a herbalist's cure-all!) and valerian used to be included.
Wild bullaces and sour cherries can also be used
to make equally fine liqueurs.*

250 g (8 oz) damsons
50 g (2 oz/¼ cup) caster sugar
600 ml (1 pint/2½ cups) gin

Wash and dry the damsons, removing any stalks. Prick all over with a silver needle or fork and place with the sugar in a large empty gin bottle or Kilner jar. Pour in the gin and seal tightly, then shake the bottle to dissolve the sugar. Leave in a cool, dark place for 3 weeks, shaking every day, then store undisturbed for 3 months at least. (Damson gin is really at its best after a year.)

Strain through two layers of scalded muslin into a clean bottle before drinking. The remaining damsons are quite delicious too; eat them with cream or yoghurt as a treat at Christmas.

Serve a nip of damson gin with slices of Borrowdale tea bread (see page 133) or seed wigs (see page 128) to warm up visiting carol-singers on Christmas Eve. (Makes about 600 ml [1 pint/2½ cups])

Variations

DAMSON VODKA

Make as before, substituting vodka for gin. Damson vodka has a cleaner, fruitier flavour, but is just as rich.

DAMSON WHISKY

Make as before, substituting whisky for gin. This is the drink recommended by the growers of those famous damsons in the Lyth Valley.

SLOE GIN OR VODKA

The sloe is the fruit of the blackthorn, common in hedgerows and open woodland throughout Britain. There are numerous recipes for sloe gin, which is better known than damson gin, and is traditionally opened with great ceremony at Christmas time.

Gather the fruits after the first frost, or put them in the freezer overnight to soften the skins. Make in the same way as damson gin or vodka.

HAWTHORN FLOWER LIQUEUR

*Hawthorn flowers, or may, can be picked
during May and early summer from most hedgerows
in Britain. They make a fine liqueur with an almond
flavour. Cut the pink or white flowers off the bush with
scissors, trying to avoid the thin stalks.
Hawthorn flower liqueur is also useful
when making any pudding or cake which calls for a
little brandy as a flavouring.*

Hawthorn flowers, stripped from their stalks
2 (3 US) tablespoons sugar
300 ml (½ pint/1¼ cups) brandy

Check that the flowers are clean and insect-free, then pack loosely into a jar to half fill it. Sprinkle over the sugar and fill up the jar with brandy. Seal with a lid and leave in a warm place for at least 3 months, shaking the jar fairly frequently during the first 2 weeks to dissolve the sugar.

Strain through two layers of scalded muslin into an empty brandy bottle. Seal tightly and drink when you wish. (Makes 300 ml [½ pint/1¼ cups])

LAMBSWOOL

In the past, lambswool was the standard English Christmas drink, carried by carol singers in the wassail bowl. Beatrix Potter describes the custom in her longer book, published in 1929, The Fairy Caravan.

*'Wassail, wassail! to our town!
The bowl is white, and the ale is brown;
The bowl is made of the rosemary tree, and so is
the ale, of the good barlee.'*

Beatrix and Willie always gave a warm welcome to the carollers when they came to sing at Castle Cottage.

1.8 litres (3 pints/3¾ US pints) strong brown ale
450 ml (¾ pint/scant 2 cups) sweet white wine
5 cm (2 in) piece of cinnamon stick
¼ whole nutmeg, grated
½ teaspoon ground ginger
2 strips of lemon rind
4 baked eating apples
Soft dark brown sugar, to taste

Heat the ale, wine, spices and lemon rind in a large pan. Skin the apples and remove the pulp. Mash it well in a very large bowl. Remove the cinnamon stick and lemon rind from the hot ale, then pour it over the apple pulp. Mix well, then push through a sieve. Add sugar to taste and reheat.

Serve steaming from a punch bowl or jug into warmed mugs or glasses and drink with Cumberland rum nickies (see page 113), warm seed wigs (see page 128) or slices of Borrowdale tea bread (see page 133). (Serves 6)

NETTLE BEER

Stinging nettles were once widely used by country people to make a light and refreshing beer, a little like ginger beer. The plant is rich in minerals, including iron, and is believed to lower blood pressure and blood-sugar levels. Pick the nettles (wearing gloves of course) early in the season when they are about 1–2.5 cm (1–2 in) high. Failing that, pick the top 1–2.5 cm (1–2 in) or so of pale young leaves from established plants, but forget about them after the end of May, when the leaves coarsen and turn bitter.

700 g (1½ lb) young stinging nettles
12 g (½ oz) dried whole root ginger, bruised
Thinly pared rind and juice of 2 large lemons
4.8 litres (8 pints/5 US quarts) cold water
450 g (1 lb/2 cups) soft light brown sugar
25 g (1 oz) cream of tartar
25 g (1 oz) fresh yeast or 1 tablespoon dried yeast or 2 (¼-oz) pkgs US active dry yeast

Put the young nettles into a large pan with the ginger, the thinly pared lemon rind and the water. Bring to the boil, then simmer for 30 minutes.

Place the lemon juice, sugar and cream of tartar in a clean container, such as a plastic bucket, and strain on the nettle liquid, pressing the nettles down well in the sieve to extract as much juice as possible. Stir until the sugar dissolves, then leave to cool to blood temperature. Stir in yeast, or sprinkle on top if dried.

Cover the beer and leave it to ferment in the airing cupboard or a warm place for 3 days, or until fermentation has stopped. Syphon off the beer, leaving all the yeasty sediment in the bottom of the container. Pour the beer into clean bottles and add ½ teaspoon brown sugar for each 600 ml (1 pint/2½ cups) to get the beer working again. Seal the bottles with well-fitting caps and stand in a cool place for about a week until the beer is clear.

When you drink the beer, pour it out carefully, leaving the sediment in the bottom of the bottles. (Makes about 4.8 litres [8 pints/5 US quarts])

Ginger beer, mulled elderberry wine and Hawkshead seed wigs (see page 128 for recipe)

GINGER BEER

2 large lemons
50 g (2 oz) fresh root ginger or 25 g (1 oz) dried whole
root ginger, bruised
1 teaspoon cream of tartar
450 g (1 lb/2 cups) granulated sugar
4.8 litres (8 pints/5 US quarts) boiling water
25 g (1 oz) fresh yeast or 1 tablespoon dried yeast or 2
(¼-oz) pkgs US active dry yeast

Wash the lemons, then pare off the rind thinly. Remove all the white pith from the lemons and discard it. Cut the lemon flesh into thin slices, removing and discarding the pips, then put the lemon peel and slices into a large bowl with the ginger, cream of tartar and sugar. Pour over the boiling water, stir, then leave to cool to blood temperature. Stir in the fresh yeast, or sprinkle on the top if using dried, then cover with a clean cloth and leave in a warm place for 24 hours to ferment. Skim off the froth with a slotted spoon, then strain. Pour into clean strong beer, champagne or fizzy drink bottles which have firm caps with metal springs.

Leave in a cool, dark place for 3 days, when the ginger beer will be ready to drink. (Makes 4.8 litres [8 pints/5 US quarts])

Variation

MULLED GINGER BEER

Follow the recipe for mulled elderberry wine (see page 143), using ginger beer, but omit the sugar.

MULLED ELDERBERRY WINE

*Elderberries grow in abundance in Lakeland
and have always been popular for making into wine.
The fruit is ready for picking in early autumn, when
the clusters hang downwards and can easily be broken
off by hand. Mind you, you have to beat the birds.
Any red wine can be used in this recipe,
although elderberry is particularly good.*

1 bottle elderberry wine
2 (3 US) tablespoons caster sugar
Thinly pared rind of 1 orange
4 whole cloves
5 cm (2 in) piece of cinnamon stick
1 blade mace
6 orange slices

Put the wine and sugar into a large pan. Heat very gently until the sugar has dissolved. Add the orange rind and spices and bring slowly to simmering point. Simmer for 5–10 minutes, then strain into a warmed jug. Pour into warmed glasses, put a slice of orange into each glass and serve. The wine should not be too hot, or it is impossible to hold or to drink.

Serve with warm seed wigs (see page 128) or buttered Borrowdale tea bread (see page 133) at Christmas time. (Serves 6)

ELDERFLOWER CHAMPAGNE

*Elderflower champagne has been a favourite
summer drink with country people for many years.
It is light, fragrant and extremely fizzy and I am always
amazed that such a superb drink can be
made from such simple ingredients and in just 3
weeks. This particular recipe was given to me by an
elderly lady in my village in Cornwall; a strict Methodist
and, like Beatrix Potter, a teetotaller. She insisted that it was
non-alcoholic – I believed her!
Pick the elderflowers on a dry sunny day when
the flowers are almost fully open and remember to use
strong beer, champagne and fizzy drink bottles, preferably
with old-fashioned wire stoppers.*

2 large handfuls of freshly gathered elderflower
heads
700 g (1½ lb) white cube sugar
2 (3 US) tablespoons white wine vinegar
1 large lemon
4.8 litres (8 pints/5 US quarts) cold water

Strip the elderflowers from their stalks and place in a large earthenware or china bowl, or jug, with the sugar and wine vinegar. Thinly pare the rind from the lemon and squeeze out the juice, then add rind and juice to the bowl. Pour on the water, cover with a clean cloth and leave to steep for 24 hours. Strain through scalded muslin, then pour into clean screw-top bottles. Seal and allow to stand for 2–3 weeks, when it is ready to drink.

Try pouring a little elderflower champagne over strawberries, raspberries or peaches just before serving and decorate with a few scented rose-petals – ambrosia. (Makes 4.8 litres [8 pints/5 US quarts])

ELDERFLOWER SYRUP

*This elderflower drink really is non-alcoholic. Again, pick
the flowers on a dry sunny day when they are almost in full
bloom. Undiluted, elderflower syrup makes a good base for
fruit salads.*

1 kg (2½ lb/5 cups) granulated sugar
1.8 litres (3 pints/3¾ US pints) cold water
50 g (2 oz) citric acid
2 large oranges
2 large lemons
About 20 large elderflower heads
Lemon slices, to garnish
Tiny sprigs of lemon balm and a few fresh
elderflowers, to garnish

Place the sugar and water in a large saucepan and heat gently until all the sugar has dissolved. Bring to the boil and continue boiling rapidly for 5 minutes. Pour this sugar syrup into a large earthenware or china bowl and stir in the citric acid. Roughly chop the oranges and lemons and add to the bowl with the elderflower heads.

Cover with a clean cloth and leave to steep for 4 days, stirring every morning and every evening. Strain through scalded muslin and pour into clean screw-top bottles. Dilute with sparkling spring water or soda water and serve garnished with lemon slices, tiny sprigs of lemon balm and a few fresh elderflowers. (Makes about 1.8 litres [3 pints/3¾ US pints])

Variation

APPLE AND ELDERFLOWER PUNCH

Add elderflower cordial to apple juice, to taste, and dilute with lemonade. Serve chilled and garnished with sprigs of mint, slices of apple and lemon and, if possible, a few borage or bergamot flowers.

OLD-FASHIONED LEMONADE

*The annual Christmas party given by Beatrix and her
husband for local Sawrey children is remembered well by
Farmer Postlethwaite's daughter, Amanda. It was held at
Castle Cottage on a Saturday afternoon from 3pm–6pm.
All the furniture was cleared out of the sitting room and
the party started off with folk dancing with Willie playing
the pianola.
Tea was laid out in the kitchen and the children helped
themselves. The occasion must have been a little like Jenny
Ferret's mouse-party in* The Fairy Caravan, *with 'cake,
tea, bread and butter, and jam and raisins for a tea party;
and comfits, and currants, lemonade, biscuits and toasted
cheese for a dance supper to follow.'*

3 large, preferably thin-skinned, lemons
75 g (3 oz/6 US tablespoons) caster or brown sugar,
or honey
1 litre (2 pints/5 cups) boiling water
Ice cubes
2–3 sprigs of fresh lemon balm, mint or rosemary,
to garnish
2–3 lemon slices, to garnish
Borage flowers, to garnish

Wash the lemons and cut them into small cubes,
reserving all the juice. Put the flesh and juice into a
large earthenware or china jug with the sugar. Pour
over the boiling water and leave for 15–30 minutes,
or until the flavour is strong, but not bitter. Strain the
lemonade and chill in the fridge.

An hour before it is wanted, pour the lemonade
into a clean jug with plenty of ice cubes and garnish
with sprigs of herbs, lemon slices and borage
flowers.

The strength of lemons varies considerably and it
may be advisable to dilute the lemonade, particularly
for children who may not have tasted the flavour of
real lemonade before and could be put off if it is
served too strong. Dilute with bottled still spring
water. (Makes about 1 litre [2 pints/1¼ US quarts])

Variations

FIZZY LEMONADE

Make as before, but add only 450 ml (¾ pint/scant 2
cups) boiling water. Dilute as required with sparkling spring water or soda water.

BURNET LEMONADE

The leaves of the herb salad burnet have a fresh
cucumber taste, ideal for wine cups and cooling
summer drinks. Add 2 (3 US) tablespoons chopped
salad burnet leaves to the lemons and sugar, then
pour over the boiling water. Continue as before.

ORANGE AND LEMON SQUASH

*Beatrix Potter allowed Girl Guides to camp
in her fields and farm buildings in the Lake District.
She enjoyed their camp-fire tea parties and sing-songs.*

4 large juicy oranges
2 large lemons
1 litre (2 pints/5 cups) boiling water
900 g (2 lb/4 cups) sugar
25 g (1 oz) citric acid
12 g (½ oz) tartaric acid
Sprigs of fresh mint, lemon balm or borage,
to garnish
Slices of orange and lemon, to garnish

Mince the oranges and lemons or chop them up in a
food processor. Place in a large bowl and add the
boiling water. Stir in the sugar until completely
dissolved, then cover with a clean cloth and leave to
steep for 24 hours. Then add the acid and strain
through scalded muslin at least 3 times until clear.
Pour into clean sterilised bottles.

Dilute with iced spring or soda water and serve
garnished with sprigs of herbs and orange and lemon
slices. (Makes about 1.5 litres [2½ pints/1½ US quarts])

*W*ILD RASPBERRY CORDIAL

Beatrix Potter was very keen on soft fruits
and planted raspberries, loganberries, gooseberries,
strawberries, and currants amongst the flowers in her
garden at Hill Top. Like most country women of the time,
she would have made soft fruit cordials,
which usually found their place in the medicine
cupboard to ease sore throats and ward off winter colds.
They are, however, wonderful served ice-cold, to restore
stamina on a hot summer's day, or steaming hot,
to warm you up after a brisk walk in the snow.
Wild raspberries can still be found in
the Lake District and Scotland, but garden raspberries
can be used, of course.

450 g (1 lb/1 quart) very ripe wild or garden
raspberries
600 ml (1 pint/2½ cups) wine or cider vinegar
450 g (1 lb/2 cups) sugar to each 600 ml (1 pint/2½
cups) fruit vinegar

Pick over the raspberries and remove any leaves and
stalks, but do not wash. Place in a large china bowl
and break up the fruit a little with the back of a
wooden spoon. Pour over the vinegar and cover with
a clean cloth. Leave in a sunny place, or in the airing
cupboard, for 5–7 days, just stirring occasionally.

Strain through a scalded jelly bag and measure the
liquid. Put into a pan with the appropriate amount of
sugar and heat gently until all the sugar has dissolved. Bring to the boil and boil rapidly for 10
minutes, then cool a little. Pour into clean bottles and
seal tightly with vinegar-proof tops.

Stir a spoonful into a glass of iced spring or sparkling water for a refreshing summer drink, or dilute
with boiling water for a warming drink in winter.

Fruit cordials are also useful undiluted as sauces
for plain sponge, batter and milk puddings, for
pouring over ice-creams, for sweet-and-sour sauces
and for adding to casseroles and gravies – particularly with lamb, pork, goose, duck and game. (Makes
about 900 ml [1½ pints/3¾ cups])

Variations

*E*LDERBERRY ROB

Use elderberries instead of raspberries and make as
before. Stir 1 teaspoon honey and a pinch of ground
cinnamon into a glass of hot water, then stir in 1–2
(1–3 US) tablespoons elderberry cordial. This makes a
lovely warming drink, especially if you have a cold or
sore throat.

*R*ASPBERRY VINEGAR

Steep the fruit in the vinegar as before, then strain
and bottle before boiling up with the sugar. (Malt
vinegar is traditional, but wine or cider vinegar is
more to our taste today.) Raspberry vinegar has
become very fashionable because of its remarkable
fruity fragrance, and makes very successful salad
dressings and sauces. Use undiluted.

Other soft fruits, such as blackcurrants, blackberries, strawberries and elderberries are equally good
for making fruit vinegars.

Raspberries can be used to flavour a variety of hot and cold drinks

HERB TEAS

Many aromatic leaves, seeds, roots and flowers – both fresh and dried – make deliciously flavoured teas. Beatrix Potter owned an early edition of Gerard's Herbal *and knew many plant remedies, including the benefits of herb teas. She, or rather, old Mrs Rabbit, doses Peter Rabbit with camomile tea to settle his stomach after over-eating in Mr McGregor's garden. In* The Fairy Caravan, *the cat Mary Ellen consults 'old Gerard in the big calfskin book' and makes 'nice rue tea in a little china cuppy cuppy, for poor sick piggy-wiggies with tummyakies' – in other words, Paddy Pig, who has been eating too many toadstools.*

Although Peter Rabbit hid under the bedclothes and Paddy Pig swallowed the tea 'under protest', most herb teas are very pleasant to drink. They can be taken warm in winter and chilled in summer and can replace ordinary tea at meal-times, or be drunk as a soothing nightcap. Try camomile, mint, lime, peppermint, nettle, rosehip, rose petal or lemon verbena.

For leaf or flower tea

1 teaspoon dried or 1 tablespoon fresh
leaves or flowers
1 cup boiling water
Honey or sugar, to sweeten (optional)

If using fresh leaves or flowers, crush them first. Put the leaves or flowers in a small warm teapot. Pour over the boiling water and leave to stand for 3–5 minutes, depending on the herb. (Overlong steeping can ruin the delicate flavour of many herb teas, so you will have to experiment.) Strain into a cup and sweeten if you wish before drinking.

For iced tea, make in the same way, strain, cover and leave to cool in the fridge.

For seed and root tea

1 tablespoon seeds or root, crushed
2 cups boiling water

The seeds or roots have to be ground in a pestle and mortar just before use. Then place them in a pan with the boiling water. Simmer gently until the water is reduced by half, strain and drink. (Serves 1)

KENDAL MINT CAKE

Kendal mint cake is not a cake, but a delicious candy-like sweetmeat known all over Britain and sold in health and sports shops in Europe, the USA and Canada. It is ideal for eating under strenuous climbing conditions and was amongst the provisions carried by Sir Edmund Hillary and Sherpa Tensing on that famous expedition to Everest. When they reached the summit on 29 May, 1953, Sir Edmund wrote: 'We sat on the snow and looked at the country far below us . . . we nibbled Kendal mint cake.' Perhaps in The Tale of Pigling Bland *the peppermints that Aunt Pettitoes gave Pigling Bland and his brother Alexander to sustain them on their long journey from Hill Top farm to 'market in Lancashire' were Kendal mint cake.*

400 g (14 oz/1¾ cups) white or soft brown sugar
50 g (2 oz/⅓ cup) glucose powder
150 ml (¼ pint/⅔ cup) milk
½ teaspoon peppermint essence

Put the sugar, glucose and milk into a saucepan and heat very gently until the sugar has completely dissolved. Bring to the boil and boil rapidly until 'soft ball' stage is reached (120 °C, 240 °F on a sugar thermometer). To test without a thermometer, place a small drop of the syrup into cold water. When rolled with the fingers, the syrup should form a soft ball.

Remove from the heat, add the peppermint essence and beat well until smooth and slightly setting, but still liquid. Pour into an oiled 20 cm (8 in) square tin, or to a depth of about 6 mm (¼ in). Mark into large squares with a knife just before the mint cake sets and break up the cake when cold.
(Makes about 450 g [l lb])

WESTMORLAND TREACLE TOFFEE APPLES

Beatrix Potter wrote a longer book for children, The Fairy Caravan, *which tells of a magical circus touring the countryside. A number of animals appear in the story, including Miss Louisa Pussycat who had started a mouse seminary at Thimble Hall. While she was out shopping, the naughty mice made 'Toffee! Mouse toffee! Toffee with lemon in it.' Louisa threatened to 'bake the whole seminary in a pasty!'*

There are many ways of making toffee in Lakeland and every part of the area seems to have its own variation. Many recipes use black treacle, which is a traditional ingredient because of the trade between Cumbrian ports and the West Indies, but children often prefer golden syrup. This particular version comes from Windermere.

450 g (1 lb/2 cups) demerara sugar
1 tablespoon golden syrup or black treacle
50 g (2 oz/¼ cup) butter
2 teaspoons malt vinegar
150 ml (¼ pint/⅔ cup) cold water
6–8 medium-sized Cox's Orange apples
6–8 wooden sticks

Heat the sugar, syrup or treacle, butter, vinegar and water very gently in a large heavy-based saucepan until all the sugar has dissolved. Bring to the boil and boil rapidly for about 5 minutes until the 'hard ball' stage is reached, or the temperature reaches 140 °C (280 °F) on a sugar thermometer. (To test the toffee without a thermometer, drop a little into a saucer of cold water; if it separates into threads which become hard but not brittle, the toffee is ready.)

Wipe the apples and push the sticks into the cores. Dip the apples into the toffee until evenly coated, then twirl around for a few seconds to allow the excess toffee to drip off. Stand on an oiled or buttered baking sheet or waxed paper and leave to set. Do not keep for more than 1 day. (Makes 6–8)

Variation

WESTMORLAND TREACLE TOFFEE

Make as before, then pour the toffee into a well-buttered baking tray so that it is not more than 6 cm (¼ in) thick. While the toffee is setting, mark deeply into small squares with a sharp knife. Leave to set completely, then turn out and break into pieces. Store in an airtight tin.

Illustration from The Fairy Caravan

Preserves

HILL TOP GARDEN JAM

The large gardens designed by Capability Brown at Camfield Place in Hertford, home of Beatrix Potter's grandmother, were paradise for young children. Beatrix adored Camfield, and based Birds' Place in The Fairy Caravan *on those grounds. 'Currant and gooseberry bushes had run wild in the thicket; they bore the sweetest little berries that the blackbirds loved. No one pruned the bushes, or netted them against the birds; no one except the birds gathered the strawberries that were scarcely larger than wild white strawberries of the woods.'*
In later years she was able to plant out her own garden at Hill Top, much to her delight. It was 'a regular old-fashioned farm garden, with a box hedge round the flower bed, and moss roses and pansies and blackcurrants and strawberries.' I am sure she would be extremely pleased that the National Trust are busy replanting her garden as it used to be, with the help of details from her letters, old photographs and drawings from her little books. Hardly anything can bring back memories of warm summer days in the garden more potently than this heavenly jam – ideal for a 'cream tea'.

450 g (1 lb/1 quart) redcurrants
450 g (1 lb/1 quart) blackcurrants
450 g (1 lb/1 quart) strawberries
450 g (1 lb/1 quart) raspberries
1 large, dark-red and heavily-scented rose
A little butter or glycerine
150 ml (¼ pint/⅔ cup) cold water
1.8 kg (4 lb/8 cups) granulated or preserving sugar, warmed

Wash the currants and remove from their stems with a fork. Pick over, hull and quarter the strawberries and pick over the raspberries. Remove the petals from the rose and snip off the white bases of the petals. Discard any green inner petals.

Rub the base of a large pan with a little butter or glycerine, then simmer the blackcurrants and red-currants in the water for 15–20 minutes, or until tender. Add the remaining fruits and simmer for a few minutes until they too are tender. Stir in the sugar over a very gentle heat until completely dissolved, then bring to the boil and add the rose petals. Boil rapidly until setting point is reached. The first indication of this is that high frothing stops and the boiling sounds noisy, with heavy plopping bubbles. This can happen within 3–5 minutes or take as long as 15–20 minutes. To test for setting, remove the pan from the heat and put a little jam on a saucer which has been in the ice-box of the fridge. Cool quickly in the fridge, then run your little finger through the centre. If setting point has been reached, the jam will crinkle slightly and a channel will remain through the middle.

You can also use a sugar thermometer, which should be dipped into hot water immediately before and after use. Stir the jam, insert the thermometer and secure to the side of the pan. A good set should be obtained when the temperature reaches 110°C (220°F).

Once setting point has been reached, skim off any frothy scum that may be on the surface, then pour into perfectly clean, dry and warmed jars, filling them to the brim to allow for any shrinkage. Cover the surface of the jam immediately with waxed paper discs, then seal tightly with cellophane or plastic lids. (This can also be done when the jam is cold.) Wipe the outside of the filled jars while hot with a hot, damp cloth, label and store in a cool, dry, airy place. (If you store jam or jelly in damp conditions, a mould may develop on the top.) (Makes about 2.7 kg [6 lb])

BLACKBERRY JAM

1 kg (2¼ lb/generous 2 quarts) blackberries
A little butter or glycerine
4 tablespoons (⅓ cup) cold water
2 medium lemons
1 kg (2¼ lb/4½ cups) granulated or preserving sugar,
warmed

Pick over the blackberries and if necessary, rinse them briefly. Rub the base of a pan with a little butter or glycerine to stop the fruit from sticking and from forming unnecessary scum. Put the blackberries in the pan with the water.

Thinly pare the rind from the lemons, using a potato peeler, and squeeze the juice, reserving the pips. Tie the rind and pips in a muslin bag and add to the pan with the lemon juice. Bring to the boil, then simmer gently for about 20 minutes until the fruit is very soft and the mixture is thick. Cool a little and remove the muslin bag, then rub the fruit through a fine nylon sieve to remove the seeds.

Return the fruit pulp to the cleaned pan and add the warmed sugar. Stir over a gentle heat until the sugar has completely dissolved, then bring to the boil and boil rapidly until setting point is reached (see previous recipe). Pot and cover in the usual way, as described in the previous recipe.

Hill Top garden jam and blackberry jam are both delicious spread on fresh scones or West Country splits and served with lashings of clotted or whipped cream. (Makes about 1.35 kg [3 lb])

Variation

BRAMBLE, ELDERBERRY AND HAZELNUT JAM

Use equal quantities of blackberries and elderberries and, if liked, include 50 g (2 oz/½ cup) roughly chopped hazelnuts. Continue as before.

PEAR AND GINGER JAM

Beatrix Potter made pear jam, probably from pears grown in the orchard at Hill Top or at Troutbeck Park, described in The Fairy Caravan. *'The orchard which gives Codlin Croft Farm its name is a long rambling strip of ground, with old bent pear trees and apple trees that bear ripe little summer pears in August and sweet codlin apples in September.'*
In this recipe, ginger has been added to give extra flavour to the jam, but it may be omitted if you prefer.

1.2 kg (2½ lb) firm cooking pears, after peeling
and coring
A little butter or glycerine
300 ml (½ pint/1¼ cups) cold water
About 2 teaspoons ground ginger
900 g (2 lb/4 cups) granulated or preserving
sugar, warmed

Tie the peel and cores from the pears in a muslin bag. Rub the base of a preserving pan with a little butter or glycerine, and put the prepared pears, muslin bag and water into the pan. Stir in the ginger and simmer very gently for about 30 minutes until a very smooth pulp forms. (If the pears are very hard they may need cooking for an extra 15 minutes with a little more water.)

Remove the muslin bag, then add the warmed sugar. Stir over a very gentle heat until the sugar has completely dissolved, then bring to the boil. Boil rapidly until setting point is reached and then pot and cover in the usual way (see page 152). (Makes about 1.35 kg [3 lb])

Variation

PEAR OR APPLE AND CLOVE JAM

Include 9–12 whole cloves in the muslin bag with the parings and continue as before, omitting the ginger. Cooking apples can be used instead of pears to make both these jams.

ℛED GOOSEBERRY JAM

*Ripe gooseberry jam is preferred by many
people for its aromatic perfume, but because the fruit
is more mature, the seeds are larger. If you wish, the hot
jam can be rubbed through a fine-meshed sieve before
potting it, to remove the seeds.*

1.35 kg (3 lb/3 quarts) red gooseberries
A little butter or glycerine
225 ml (7½ fl oz/scant 1 cup) cold water
1.35 kg (3 lb/6 cups) granulated or preserving
sugar, warmed

Rinse and top and tail the gooseberries, using scissors. Rub the base of a preserving pan with a little butter or glycerine, then put in the fruit with the water. Cook over a gentle heat for about 15 minutes, stirring occasionally, until the gooseberries are soft, then add the warmed sugar and stir over a gentle heat until the sugar is completely dissolved. Bring to the boil and boil rapidly until setting point is reached (see page 152). Remove from the heat and skim off any scum with a slotted spoon. Strain through a sieve if you wish, then pot and cover (see page 152).

Spread on hot, buttered crumpets, muffins and scones, or on fresh homemade wholemeal bread. Red gooseberry jam also makes a delicious spread for a plain sponge or chocolate cake. (Makes about 2.25 kg [5 lb])

Variations

ℊREEN GOOSEBERRY JAM

Hard, immature green gooseberries have the advantage of containing much smaller seeds, but the fruit must be simmered in 450 ml (¾ pint/scant 2 cups) cold water for about 30 minutes, until soft, before adding the sugar.

ℊOOSEBERRY AND ELDERFLOWER JAM

Pick the flowers from the stalks of 5 heads of elderflowers. Check that they are insect-free, but do not wash, then roughly chop the flowers. Simmer with the gooseberries before adding the sugar.

ʃEVILLE ORANGE MARMALADE

Porridge, usually followed by eggs and bacon, brown bread, 'young churn butter' (farm butter) and homemade marmalade, were on the breakfast menu at Castle Cottage. Even during the First World War, Beatrix was able to get hold of oranges for marmalade, as we know from a wartime letter. 'I was able to make some marmalade – there was a shipload of oranges at a port going to waste, so adults were allowed a few . . .'
Try spreading marmalade on hot buttered muffins instead of toast. Ribby Pussy-cat served this dish when she entertained her friend Duchess, a 'genteel and elegant little dog', in The Tale of The Pie and The Patty-Pan. *Ribby bought the marmalade from her Cousin Tabitha Twitchit's shop (based on a building in Hawkshead).*

900 g (2 lb) Seville oranges
1 sweet orange
1 lemon
2 litres (4 pints/2½ US quarts) cold water
1.8 kg (4 lb/8 cups) granulated or preserving
sugar, warmed

Wash and scrub the oranges and lemon. Cut them in half, squeeze out the juice and pour into a preserving pan or large saucepan. Add the water to the pan. Place the pips and any odd pieces of pith sticking to the squeezer on a piece of muslin, then slice the orange and lemon peel into thin shreds. As you cut, add the shreds to the pan of water so that they don't dry up. Any pips and spare pith should be added to the muslin, because they contain a lot of pectin.

Tie up the pips and pith loosely in the muslin to form a bag and tie on to the handle of the pan so that it is suspended in the water. Bring the contents of the pan to the boil, then simmer gently for 1½–2 hours until the peel is very soft. It should disintegrate when squeezed between the fingers. Remove and discard the muslin bag, squeezing it well.

Remove the pan from the heat and gradually stir in the warmed sugar. Make sure it is completely dissolved before returning the pan to the heat and bringing back to the boil. Boil rapidly for 15–20 minutes until setting point is reached (see page 152). (While citrus fruits contain plenty of pectin and therefore have a good setting quality, the setting point is quickly passed, so test carefully and don't boil for too long.)

When setting point has been reached, skim the surface with a slotted spoon to prevent scum adhering to the pieces of peel. Allow the marmalade to stand for about 10 minutes, then give it a final stir to distribute the peel before potting in the usual way (see page 152). (Makes about 2.75 kg [6 lb])

Variations

SEVILLE ORANGE MARMALADE WITH WHISKY

Stir in about 1 dessertspoon whisky or brandy for each 450 g (1 lb) fruit, after setting point is reached.

SPICED SEVILLE ORANGE MARMALADE

Add 1 dessertspoon coriander seeds for each 450 g (1 lb) fruit to the muslin bag with the pips.

BLACKCURRANT JELLY

In 1922, Beatrix Potter agreed to rent the front half of the old Castle Cottage farmhouse to Daisy Hammond, the niece of her first governess. Miss Hammond and her companion, Miss Cecily Mills, were to live there for many years. The two women became great friends with the Heelises, and both households kept a neighbourly eye on each other.

Beatrix wrote to Daisy from the Women's Hospital in Liverpool after a serious operation in July, 1939, enquiring about her blackcurrants. 'I have been wondering whether anyone has picked black currants? There ought to be a picking ready (unless a bird has been shut into the net!) I should like to have some jelly made; the jam is less liked. Please take some for yourself too, there should be plenty.'

900 g (2 lb/2 quarts) blackcurrants
600 ml (1 pint/1½ cups) cold water
450 g (1 lb/2 cups) granulated or preserving sugar, warmed, to each 600 ml (1 pint/2½ cups) juice

Wash the blackcurrants and strip them from their stalks with a fork (it is not necessary to top and tail the fruit for jelly). Put the fruit into a pan with the water and simmer gently for about 40 minutes, until very soft.

Strain through a scalded jelly bag overnight. Blackcurrants have a high setting quality, so you can boil the fruit twice. Reserve the juice on one side, then return the pulp in the jelly bag to a pan. Pour over 300 ml (½ pint/1¼ cups) water and bring to the boil, then simmer gently for a further 40 minutes. Strain through the jelly bag again overnight.

Next day, mix the two lots of juice together and measure the quantity of liquid. Add the appropriate amount of warmed sugar and stir over a very gentle heat until the sugar has completely dissolved. Bring to the boil and boil rapidly without stirring until setting point is reached (see page 152). Skim off any scum with a slotted spoon, then pot and cover in the usual way (see page 152).

Spread on hot buttered scones, muffins and bread or eat as an accompaniment to rich meats, poultry and game.

Variations

SPICED BLACKCURRANT JELLY

Use the same recipe as before, but add 1 level teaspoon mixed spice to each 600 ml (1 pint/2½ cups) juice. Stir it in with the sugar. This jelly is particularly suitable for serving with cold meats.

BLACKCURRANT AND REDCURRANT JELLY

Use equal quantities of blackcurrants and redcurrants and continue as before.

BLACKCURRANT OR BLACKCURRANT AND REDCURRANT JELLY WITH PORT

When setting point has been reached, remove the pan from the heat. Stir in 3 tablespoons (¼ cup) port.

CRAB APPLE AND ROSE GERANIUM JELLY

*Beatrix Potter's journal entry for
20 August 1892 records a minor domestic accident
during the family's summer holiday at Heath Park, Birnam.
As she came out of a shop, her mother caught
her heel and fell, cutting her elbow to the bone. Beatrix
went with her to see the local medical man, a Dr Culbard,
'who was kind and very fat and snuffy'.
After the visit they all had tea, 'Dr Culbard tucking in
his table-napkin by way of a bib, and cutting a great slice
of bread and apple jelly'.
Beatrix made crab apple jelly herself when
she was living at Castle Cottage, using tiny rosy-cheeked
apples gathered from the orchards at Hill
Top and Castle Cottage Farm. It is the clearest, most
brilliant of jellies and can be flavoured with scented leaves,
herbs, lemon rind or spices.*

1.8 kg (4 lb) crab apples or tart cooking apples
1 litre (2 pints/5 cups) cold water
8–12 rose geranium leaves
450 g (1 lb/2 cups) granulated or preserving sugar,
warmed, to each 600 ml (1 pint/2½ cups) juice

Wash the apples and chop them up roughly, including the peel and cores. Put in a preserving pan with the water and geranium leaves. Simmer gently for 25-30 minutes, or until very soft and pulpy. Strain through a scalded jelly bag overnight.

Next day, measure the juice and put back into the cleaned pan. Heat gently, stirring in the appropriate amount of warmed sugar until completely dissolved. Bring to the boil, then boil rapidly for about 10 minutes, or until setting point is reached (see page 152). Take the pan off the heat and skim the surface with a slotted spoon. Pot and cover in the usual way (see page 152).

Spread on 'a great slice of bread', as Dr Culbard did, or put on scones, muffins and oatcakes. The jelly makes a delicious filling for sponges and cakes, and can be eaten with ham, pork, goose, duck or lamb.

BRAMBLE JELLY

*Blackberry-picking is one of the most
delightful pastimes on a warm late summer or autumn
afternoon. Beatrix Potter described the blackberry in her
journal as 'a kindly berry, it ripens in the
rain' and is free to everyone. You don't have to
live in the countryside to have access to the fruit, but
do be careful to avoid those berries growing by the side of
very busy roads.
We know that, like most country people,
Beatrix and Willie Heelis enjoyed bramble jelly
for tea. They lived simply at Castle Cottage, going
their own ways and not getting under each other's feet.
Margaret Lane, in A Tale of Beatrix Potter, speaks of 'a
law book and papers and deed-boxes at one
end of the dining-room, bramble jelly and toasted
teacakes at the other.'*

900 g (2 lb/2 quarts) blackberries
150 ml (¼ pint/⅔ cup) cold water
4 tablespoons (⅓ cup) lemon juice
400 g (14 oz/1¾ cups) granulated or preserving sugar,
warmed, to each 600 ml (1 pint/2½ cups) juice

Pick over the blackberries, removing any stalks and leaves. Try not to wash the fruit unless absolutely necessary. Put in a pan with the water and simmer very gently for about 25–30 minutes, until very soft. Strain through a scalded jelly bag overnight.

Next day, measure the juice and put in a large pan with the lemon juice. Add the appropriate amount of warmed sugar and heat very gently, stirring until the sugar has completely dissolved. Bring to the boil and boil rapidly until setting point is reached (see page 152). Skim off any scum, then pot and cover in the usual way (see page 152).

Eat as an accompaniment to rich meats, such as mutton, pork, venison, hare, sausages, ham, duck and goose, or spread on warm scones, muffins, oatcakes and fresh bread. Bramble jelly is also useful as a glaze for pies, flans and cheesecakes. It can be made with the same variations as blackcurrant jelly.

TULLYTHWAITE SAGE JELLY

I was given this recipe by Janet Greenwood who, with her husband, runs Tullythwaite House in the scattered village of Underbarrow, near Kendal. The restaurant in the sixteenth century farmhouse is famous for its English food made from local produce, and Janet serves this sage jelly with the Christmas goose. It is equally good with duck, pork, ham and sausages.

600 ml (1 pint/2½ cups) Copella apple juice or other cloudy fresh apple juice
180 ml (6 fl oz/¾ cup) white wine vinegar
4 tablespoons (¼ cup) lemon juice
450 ml (¾ pint/scant 2 cups) water
125 g (4 oz) fresh sage leaves, bruised
1.35 kg (3 lb/6 cups) granulated or preserving sugar, warmed
Few drops of green food colouring (optional)
1 bottle (227 ml/8 fl oz/1 cup) Certo (commercial liquid fruit pectin)

Place the apple juice, vinegar, lemon juice and water in a very large enamel or stainless steel saucepan. Bring to the boil, then add the sage leaves. Transfer to a china or earthenware bowl, cover with a clean cloth and leave overnight to infuse.

Next day, pour the liquid (including the leaves) back into the original, cleaned saucepan. Add the warmed sugar to the liquid with the food colouring, if using. Heat gently until the sugar has dissolved, stirring frequently, then bring to a rolling boil. Add the Certo and bring back to the boil. Boil steadily for about 3 minutes, until it has reached setting point.

Strain off the sage leaves and pot and cover in the usual way (see page 152). (Makes 5 [350-g/12-oz] jars)

Variations

Many other herbs may be used instead of sage. Try mint, rosemary, thyme, lemon balm, marjoram and basil.

Lakeland jellies from Tullythwaite House

SPICED ROWAN JELLY

The clusters of large orange-red berries from the rowan or mountain ash tree, common throughout Britain, make the most deliciously tangy jelly. It is traditionally served with mountain meats, such as grouse, venison, hare and mutton, although it is also good with other feathered game, goose, duck, pork and lamb. The Potter family would no doubt have been served rowan jelly with the venison and grouse shot by Mr Potter, Bertram and the many friends who joined them on their summer holidays in the Scottish Highlands and the Lake District.
Certainly, Beatrix made and ate rowan jelly, among other preserves, in her later years in the Lake District. A fragment of writing, at one time intended for a sequel to The Fairy Caravan, *describes Hill Top farmhouse, '"Then there is a tall wall cupboard, a shallow cupboard with many shelves, where Mistress Heelis keeps the marmalade and jam . . . thirty to forty pounds of marmalade, at this time of year," said Pippin, licking his fingers, "and strawberry jam and plum and blackberry jelly, and rowan jelly to eat with Herdwick mutton . . ."'*
Pick the rowan berries as soon as they have turned orange in early October, before the birds eat them. Break off the clusters whole from the tree by hand. They will keep for several days in the fridge. Crab or cooking apples and lemon juice must be added, because the rowan berries are low in pectin. The spices can be omitted if you wish. Traditionally, a branch of rowan with berries was hung in Cumbrian stables to protect the animals from sickness and harm.

1.8 kg (4 lb) rowan berries, picked off the stalks
900 g (2 lb) crab apples or cooking apples
5 cm (2 in) piece cinnamon stick (optional)
1 teaspoon whole cloves (optional)
Cold water, to cover
350 g (12 oz/1½ cups) granulated or preserving sugar, warmed, to each 600 ml (1 pint/2½ cups) juice, for sharp jelly, or 450 g (1 lb/2 cups) for a sweeter jelly

Wash the rowan berries and apples. Roughly chop the apples without peeling or coring, then put the berries and apples into a preserving pan or very large saucepan with the cinnamon and cloves (if you are using them). Barely cover with cold water, then bring slowly to the boil. Simmer very gently for about 30 minutes, or until the berries and apples are soft and pulpy. Strain through a scalded jelly bag overnight.

Next day, measure the juice and return it to the cleaned pan. Add the appropriate amount of warmed sugar and heat very gently, stirring frequently, until the sugar has completely dissolved. Bring to the boil and boil rapidly until setting point is reached (see page 152). Skim with a slotted spoon and pot and cover in the usual way (see page 152).

DAMSON JELLY

Beatrix made damson jelly in September, using damsons gathered from the orchards at Hill Top and Castle Farm.

1.8 kg (4 lb) damsons
900 ml (1½ pints/3¾ cups) cold water
450 g (1 lb/2 cups) granulated or preserving sugar, warmed, to each 600 ml (1 pint/2½ cups) juice

Wash the damsons well and remove any stalks. Simmer gently in the water for about 40 minutes until very soft and pulpy, stirring from time to time. The fruit can be broken up with a potato masher to help this process. (This may be done with all fruit for jellies except quinces, pears and apples, where the pressing will result in a cloudy jelly.) Strain through a scalded jelly bag overnight.

Next day, measure the juice and place in a large pan. Add the appropriate amount of warmed sugar and heat very gently until the sugar is completely dissolved. Bring to the boil and boil rapidly until setting point is reached (see page 152). Skim the surface with a slotted spoon to remove any scum, then pot and cover in the usual way (see page 152).

Spread on bread, scones, muffins and crumpets, or use as an accompaniment to lamb, mutton, ham, tongue, duck and goose.

QUINCE JELLY

There is a large old Japanese quince or japonica tree growing around the front door at Hill Top, Beatrix Potter's first Lakeland home, and the National Trust staff working there make the fruit into jelly. The ornamental quince is really grown for its showy flowers, but it still makes a very pleasant-flavoured jelly. If using japonicas or very ripe quinces, the juice of 1 lemon should be added to each 600 ml (1 pint/2½ cups) of juice, to make certain of a good set.

1.8 kg (4 lb) quinces
3 litres (6 pints/7½ US pints) cold water
450 g (1 lb/2 cups) granulated or preserving sugar, warmed, to each 600 ml (1 pint/2½ cups) juice

Wash the quinces and wipe off the soft down on their skins. Chop up roughly, including the peel and cores. Place in a preserving pan with the water and simmer very gently for about 50 minutes, or until very soft and pulpy. Strain through a scalded jelly bag overnight.

Next day, measure the juice and return to the cleaned pan. Heat very gently, stirring in the appropriate amount of warmed sugar, until completely dissolved. Bring to the boil and boil rapidly until setting point is reached (see page 152). Pot and cover in the usual way (see page 152).

Quince jelly, with its fine deep-pink colour, is extremely versatile. It is excellent with Stilton or a good Cheddar cheese and crusty homemade bread, or as an accompaniment to roast lamb, mutton or game. Serve also spread on warm buttered scones, muffins and oatcakes, use to sandwich plain sponges together, or as a glaze on fruit flans and cheesecakes.

Variation

QUINCE AND APPLE JELLY

Use equal quantities of quinces or japonicas and apples and make as before. The lemon juice can be omitted as the apple juice ensures a good set.

LEMON CURD

Lemon curd is a favourite preserve in Lakeland. It has to be made with good fresh unsalted butter – preferably straight from the farm.

Beatrix Potter took a great interest in the butter-making at Hill Top, remembering the farm butter of her childhood visits to her grandmother's home at Camfield Place. The dairy was devoted to butter and cheese production, using milk most frequently taken from Shorthorn cows. Beatrix wrote to Millie Warne in 1905 about taking the farm butter scales to the police station to be tested. They were not accurate, but Beatrix continues, 'Fortunately I have been cheating myself, the dish that held the butter had some enamel chipped off it, so we have been selling about ½ ounce over the pound. If it had been the other way round I should probably have been fined.' She was proud of her butter which did well at the Dairy Show.

250 g (8 oz/1 cup) caster sugar
Grated rind and juice of 2 large lemons
3 large eggs, well-beaten
125 g (4 oz/½ cup) unsalted butter

Place the sugar, lemon rind and juice and beaten eggs in the top of a double saucepan or in a basin standing over a saucepan of barely simmering water. Gradually add the butter, cut into little pieces, and stir over a low heat until thick – for about 15 minutes. The mixture must not boil or the eggs may curdle.

Pot and cover in the usual way (see page 152). Lemon curd will only keep for about 1 month in a dry airy cupboard, or up to 3 months in a fridge, so make a small quantity at a time. Serve spread thickly on fresh bread, toast, crumpets, muffins, scones and plain cakes, such as the Lakeland Lemon Bread on page 00, or use to fill sponges, tarts and pastries. (Makes about 675 g [1½ lb])

Variation

Substitute the following fruit for the 2 lemons and make as before: 2 large oranges and 1 lemon; or 3 limes; or 2 large grapefruit; or 3 large oranges.

PARSLEY HONEY

Beatrix Potter grew plenty of parsley in Hill Top garden and you can still see it growing there. She was also aware of the old-fashioned remedy for the relief of indigestion; Peter Rabbit felt rather sick because he had overindulged in Mr McGregor's garden, so 'went to look for some parsley'! This particular recipe is very useful because parsley that has gone to seed can be used. Parsley honey was popular during the war when ordinary honey was in short supply.

125–150 g (4–5 oz) fresh parsley
900 ml (1½ pints/3¾ cups) cold water
450 g (1 lb/2 cups) granulated or preserving sugar, warmed
1 dessertspoon vinegar or lemon juice

Wash and pick over the parsley, then chop roughly, including the stalks. Put into a pan with the water, then bring to the boil. Continue to boil gently until the water is reduced to 600 ml (1 pint/2½ cups) – about 30 minutes. Strain off this parsley water and reserve. Rinse out the pan, then pour back the parsley water. Add the warmed sugar, then heat gently until the sugar is completely dissolved. Bring to the boil, add the vinegar or lemon juice and boil slowly until a little of the mixture, when tested on a plate, is of a clear-honey consistency. This will probably take about 30 minutes. Pot and cover in the usual way (see page 152).

Spread on fresh buttered bread, scones, toast, crumpets and muffins, or use for cooking. (Makes about 900 g [2 lb])

DAMSON CHEESE

Fruit cheeses are delightful traditional country preserves, with a very thick texture. They used to be served at the end of a meal with a little port wine poured over and a spoonful of fresh cream but now they are more usually eaten as an accompaniment to meat or cheese. Damson cheese is served in Lakeland homes with lamb. Many other fruits can be used to make old-fashioned cheeses – apples, blackberries, gooseberries, grapes, loganberries, cranberries (which still grow wild in marsh areas of Lakeland), mulberries, plums, quinces and blackcurrants. As the fruit is always sieved when making a cheese, the method is useful for fruits with a lot of pips and stones.

1.4 kg (3 lb) damsons
150 ml (¼ pint/⅔ cup) cold water
450 g (1 lb/2 cups) granulated or preserving sugar, to each 600 ml (1 pint/2½ cups) fruit pulp

Wash the damsons and remove their stalks. Place in an ovenproof casserole with the water. Cover with a lid and cook in a very slow oven until tender and soft. Using a wooden spoon, press the fruit pulp through a nylon sieve and measure it.

Place the pulp in a pan and add the appropriate amount of sugar. Heat slowly, stirring until the sugar has dissolved, then bring to the boil and boil gently, stirring frequently, for 30–40 minutes. The mixture should be so thick that a wooden spoon leaves a clean line through it when drawn across the bottom of the pan, and the mixture should leave the side of the pan. Spoon into small ramekin dishes, small straight-sided jars or individual moulds which have been lightly brushed with glycerine or almond oil, so that the damson cheese can be turned out. Leave to set, then cover as usual (see page 152). Label and store in a cool, dry place for at least 3 months before using. Fruit cheeses keep well, because of their high sugar content – for about 2 years.

To serve, turn out of the jar, dish or mould and cut into slices to accompany meat, poultry, game or cheese. Damson cheese is also delicious thickly spread on wholemeal bread, or can be served with junket and milk puddings. It is particularly good served with natural yoghurt or fromage frais. (Makes about 1.4 kg [3 lb])

Variation

*D*AMSON AND MINT CHEESE

Stir 3 tablespoons (¼ cup) chopped fresh mint leaves into the fruit pulp 5 minutes before it is cooked. Serve with lamb, mutton, pork or game.

Below: Roast Herdwick lamb (see page 48 for recipe) goes well with any herb or spiced fruit jelly

*P*ICKLED RED CABBAGE

In Lakeland this sharp-flavoured, rosy pickle is the traditional accompaniment to Tatie Pot (see page 44). Beatrix would have made it regularly in the autumn. The quality of red cabbage is much improved after several frosts.

1 firm red cabbage weighing about 900 g (2 lb)
1 tablespoon salt
2 teaspoons white peppercorns
½ teaspoon allspice
2 teaspoons mustard seed
½ teaspoon blade mace
½ a stick of cinnamon
600 ml (1 pint/2½ cups) cider vinegar
1 tablespoon sugar (optional)
3 slices of raw beetroot
3 slices of onion

Discard any tough outer leaves on the cabbage, then quarter it and slice finely, including the stalk. Spread the cabbage on a large flat dish, layering it with the salt. Cover with a clean cloth and leave overnight.

Next day, tie the spices together in a small muslin bag. Place in an enamel or stainless steel pan with the vinegar and sugar, if using. Cover the pan and bring slowly to the boil. When just at boiling point, draw aside and leave for about 2 hours for the spices to flavour the vinegar.

Drain off the salt from the cabbage, then pack into clean wide-necked jars. Top each jar with a slice of raw beetroot, for colour, and a slice of onion, for flavour. Remove the muslin bag from the vinegar and pour over the cabbage, covering it well. Seal the jars tightly with vinegar-proof lids. Leave for at least 1 week before eating; it is even better after 1 month.

Pickled red cabbage is traditionally served cold with cold meats and cheese and with hot lamb dishes in Lakeland, but it may be heated up if you prefer. (Makes about 1.35 kg [3 lb])

DAMSON PICKLE

Fruit is not abundant in Lakeland, with the exception of damsons, and these are magnificent – large, black and so sweet and juicy that they can be eaten raw like grapes with local cheeses. For generations, local people have bottled them and made them into jam, jelly, curd, cheese, wine, chutney and this delicious pickle.

1 kg (2 lb/4 cups) sugar
300 ml (½ pint/1¼ cups) malt vinegar
2 kg (4 lb) damsons
1 cinnamon stick
25 g (1 oz) whole cloves
1 blade of mace

Pre-heat the oven to 180°C (350°F, gas mark 4).
Place the sugar and vinegar in an ovenproof dish. Stir well. Put into a warm oven for about 20 minutes, or until the mixture has dissolved into a syrup.

Wash and dry the damsons, discarding any stalks. Prick each one several times with a fine needle, then place in a preserving pan or very large saucepan. Pour over the syrup, add the cinnamon, cloves and mace, and bring gently to the boil. Simmer gently for 10–20 minutes, until soft but quite unbroken. Then remove the fruit with a slotted spoon and pack into clean, warm jars. Pour over the syrup and spices and cover with vinegar-proof lids when cold.

Keep the damson pickle at least 3 months before using; age improves its flavour and prepared this way, it will keep for years. Damson pickle gives an uplift to any cold meat or cheese. It is particularly good with cold pheasant and other game, also accompanied with rowan jelly (see page 159). The smoky flavour of the jelly contrasts well with the slightly sharp taste of the damsons. (Makes about 2.7 kg [6 lb])

Variation

PLUM OR GREENGAGE PICKLE

Plums, including wild plums or bullaces, and greengages can be pickled in exactly the same way.

SPICED DAMSON AND RAISIN CHUTNEY

1.35 kg (3 lb) damsons
450 g (1 lb) cooking apples, when peeled and cored
450 g (1 lb) onions, peeled
3 cloves of garlic, crushed
2 heaped teaspoons ground ginger
450 g (1 lb/3 cups) seedless raisins
450 g (1 lb/2 cups) demerara sugar
450 g (1 lb/2 cups) dark soft brown sugar
1.25 litres (2 pints/5 cups) malt vinegar
2 (3 US) tablespoons salt
1 dessertspoon whole cloves
2 small cinnamon sticks
25 g (1 oz) whole allspice berries

Wash and dry the damsons, removing any stalks, then place them in a preserving pan or very large saucepan. Cook very gently in their own juice until tender, then remove the stones. Finely chop the apples and onions and add to the pan with the garlic, ginger, raisins, sugars and vinegar. Sprinkle in the salt and stir the mixture thoroughly. Tie the cloves, cinnamon sticks and allspice berries in a small square of muslin, with a piece of thread or string long enough to suspend the bag from the pan handle into the middle of the rest of the ingredients.

Cook gently until all the sugar has dissolved, stirring frequently, then bring to the boil. Lower the heat and simmer very gently for 2–3 hours, stirring occasionally at first, then more often towards the end of the cooking time to prevent the chutney from catching on the bottom of the pan. To tell when the chutney is cooked, make a channel right across its surface with a wooden spoon; if the line shows for a few seconds without filling with vinegar, the chutney is ready.

Spoon or pour while the chutney is still hot into washed and dried jars that have been warmed in a moderate oven. Fill to the brim, then cover immediately with waxed paper circles and seal tightly with vinegar-proof lids. Leave to mature in a dry, airy place for at least 3 months before eating. Unopened,

this chutney will keep for up to 2 years. Serve with cold lamb, beef, pork, poultry, ham and cheese. (Makes about 1.8 kg [4 lb])

Variations

SPICED PLUM AND RAISIN CHUTNEY

Plums will not need the initial stewing to remove their stones – just halve them, remove the stones and continue as before.

SPICED ELDERBERRY OR BILBERRY AND RAISIN CHUTNEY

Make as before, without any initial stewing. The elderberries or bilberries can be cooked up with all the other ingredients.

HERBS AND FLOWERS

HERB VINEGARS

Like most country-lovers, Beatrix Potter was very interested in herbs and they are frequently mentioned in her stories – sage in Jemima Puddle-Duck, *camomile and rosemary for old Mrs Rabbit's teas, lavender for her rabbit-tobacco and parsley for Peter Rabbit.*

Herb vinegars are simple to make and can be used for pickling and marinades and to flavour salad dressings, mayonnaise, sauces and gravies. They can be very potent, so begin by adding a few drops to your normal vinegar until you get used to their flavour. Basil, bay, chervil, dill, fennel, lemon balm, marjoram, mint, sage, rosemary, savory, tarragon and thyme can all be used. Purple basil and sage and bronze fennel give stunning shades of ruby and burgundy to the vinegar.

Clean fresh herb leaves
Wine or cider vinegar, warmed

Bruise the leaves of your chosen herb and pack *loosely* into a glass jar with a vinegar-proof lid. Pour over the warm vinegar and fill right to the top of the jar. Seal with the lid and leave to steep on a sunny windowsill or in a warm place for 2 weeks, shaking daily. Test for flavour. If a stronger taste is required, strain off the vinegar, pour it over fresh herbs and leave to steep again. When you are satisfied with the flavour, strain the vinegar through two layers of muslin and bottle it, adding a fresh sprig of the herb for decoration and to identify.

Variations

MIXED-HERB VINEGARS

Use 2 or 3 different herbs at a time, experimenting with combinations. For herb and garlic vinegar, add several crushed cloves of garlic to the herb leaves, then pour over the vinegar. Leave to steep as before.

See also raspberry vinegar on page 146, and flower vinegars on page 170.

HERB OILS

Herbs best used for flavouring oil are basil, fennel, marjoram, mint, parsley, chives, rosemary, tarragon, thyme, savory, sage and lemon verbena. Lavender is very strongly flavoured so should be used sparingly. Bay can also be used, but the leaves should be left whole and just bruised before the oil is added. Purple sage and basil and bronze fennel give subtle burgundy shades to the oil. Olive oil is successful with some herbs, particularly basil and fennel.

Use herb oils in salad dressings, marinades and sauces and for grilling, frying, stir-frying and roasting. As with herb vinegars, start with small amounts of herb oils until their individual strengths become familiar.

4 tablespoons (⅓ cup) clean fresh herb leaves
Pinch of sea salt
450 ml (¾ pint/scant 2 cups) sunflower or safflower oil

Pound the herb leaves in a mortar with the salt. Add a little of the oil and mix together well, then pour into a clean glass jar with the remaining oil. Seal tightly and leave to steep for about 2 weeks, stirring or shaking daily. Strain into a clean bottle, adding a fresh sprig of the chosen herb to decorate and for identification. Seal tightly. (Makes 450 ml [¾ pint/ scant 2 cups])

Variations

MIXED-HERB OILS

Use 2 or 3 different herbs, steeping each one in the oil in succession. For herb and garlic oil, pound several cloves of garlic with the chosen herb and steep as before. The amount of garlic can be adjusted to your own taste. The herbs can be omitted, if you wish, to make garlic oil.

To make aromatic oils, peppercorns, red chilies, fennel seeds, juniper berries and coriander seeds may be pounded with the chosen herb.

HERB SALTS

Salt can be flavoured with herbs very successfully, using equal quantities of fresh herbs and salt. Use to flavour casseroles, soups, marinades and sauces and to season meat, fish, eggs and vegetables before or after cooking. Some of the most successful herbs to try are rosemary, thyme, mint, marjoram, sage, tarragon, lavender (use less), basil, chives, chervil, parsley and fennel. The seeds of some herbs may be used in the same way, such as fennel, dill, cumin, coriander and caraway. Crush the seeds in a mortar.

Clean fresh herb leaves
Coarse sea salt

Chop the herbs finely and place layers of herbs and salt in a small dark-coloured glass jar or a clear glass jar covered with foil, to exclude the light. Store for 2–3 weeks, then spread herbs and salt on a baking tray and dry off in a warm place. When dry, store in a clean jar. Use as it is or grind in a salt mill.

HERB RICE

Two or 3 sprigs of fresh tarragon, thyme, sage, marjoram or 2–3 fresh bay leaves will flavour a jar of long-grain rice for savoury dishes. Bay leaves are also very successful if used to flavour short grain rice for sweet rice puddings.

HERB SUGARS

The most successful herb sugars are made with rosemary, lavender, bay, lemon balm, peppermint, applemint, hyssop, bergamot, thyme and lemon verbena. They are delicious when used to make custards, fruit fools and creams, syllabubs, milk puddings, jellies, sweet soufflés, fruit salads and drinks, and can be sprinkled on the top of cakes, biscuits, pies and puddings after cooking. Savoury dishes can also benefit from a pinch of herb sugar; carrots are particularly good when glazed with butter and a little lavender sugar just before serving.

2–3 sprigs clean, fresh herb
450 g (1 lb/2 cups) caster sugar

Place the sprigs of herb in a jar and pour in the caster sugar. Seal tightly and leave to scent and flavour the sugar for 2–3 weeks, shaking every now and again. Top up with more sugar as you use it until the flavour diminishes, then start again.

Variation

Blackcurrant and rose geranium leaves are also successful for flavouring sugars.

FLOWER VINEGARS

Many of the old-fashioned, cottage-garden and wild flowers that Beatrix Potter planted – she admitted raiding every garden in Sawrey for cuttings ('I got nice things in handfuls without any shame') – can be used to flavour and colour vinegars. Some of the most successful are elderflowers, roses, marigolds, nasturtiums, primroses, cowslips, lavender (use sparingly), clover, violets and the flowers of various herbs, such as chives, rosemary, thyme, marjoram, sage and mint. Use flower vinegars to flavour salad dressings, mayonnaise, sauces and marinades. Some flower vinegars have light, delicate flavours – like elderflower, primrose, cowslip, clover and violet – while others, like lavender and herb flowers, need to be used carefully.

Clean, dry fresh flowers
White wine or cider vinegar, warmed

Gather the flowers on a dry sunny day when in full bloom and check that they are insect-free. Strip the flowers from their stems and remove the petals if using roses or marigolds (also remove the white base from rose petals), otherwise use the whole flowers. Half-fill a large glass jar with the flowers or petals, pressing them down well. Pour over the warm vinegar and fill right to the top. Cover with a vinegar-proof lid and leave to steep on a sunny windowsill or in a warm place for 2 weeks. Test the vinegar and if the flavour is satisfactory, strain through two layers of muslin into a clean bottle. Seal tightly and store in a dry airy place.

FLOWER SUGARS

Try using the flowers of herbs such as rosemary, lavender and thyme, and the petals of sweet-smelling roses, marigolds, pinks and whole elderflowers and violets to perfume sugar, which is delicious in fruit desserts like fools and creams.

CRYSTALLISED FLOWERS AND HERBS

Crystallising is an extremely pretty and effective way of preserving flowers and herbs. The flowers I have had most success with are primroses, violets, roses, daisies, mallow, pinks, carnations, pansies, borage flowers, apple, cherry, pear and quince blossom, heathers, lavender and elderflowers. Most small-leaved herbs are successful. The method of crystallising I use involves gum arabic and rose- or orange-flower water, all of which can be bought at most good chemists' or old-fashioned grocers'. The gum arabic has to soak for 24 hours, or at least overnight, before you start.

1 teaspoon gum arabic powder
1 tablespoon rose- or orange-flower water
Dry freshly gathered flowers or sprigs of herbs
Caster sugar

Put the gum arabic in a small jar and pour over the flower water. Seal tightly and leave to soak for 24 hours, shaking occasionally, until the mixture is a sticky glue.

Pick the flowers or herbs on a dry, sunny day when the dew has dried from them. The flowers must be at their best and free of insects and dust. Some are best broken up into individual petals before crystallising, such as roses and pinks. Others can be left whole, such as violets and primroses. Clusters of flowers, such as elderflowers, are best treated as a bunch and broken up after they have been crystallised.

Paint the back and front of the petals or leaves with the gum arabic solution, using a fine paintbrush. Make sure you coat them completely, as any areas left unpainted will shrivel and die. Dredge lightly all over with caster sugar and gently arrange on grease-proof paper placed over a wire cake-cooling rack. Dry off in the airing cupboard for at least 24 hours, moving them about occasionally to prevent sticking.

Store your crystallised flowers and herbs in an airtight tin between layers of greaseproof paper. Kept in a cool, dry place, they will last virtually indefinitely, but may lose their colour in time.

INDEX TO RECIPES